HANNIS TAYLOR

HANNIS TAYLOR (1851–1922)

HANNIS TAYLOR

THE NEW SOUTHERNER
AS AN AMERICAN

Tennant S. McWilliams

The University of Alabama Press
University, Alabama

Library of Congress Cataloging in Publication Data

McWilliams, Tennant S   1943–
    Hannis Taylor: the new Southerner as an American.

    Bibliography: p.
    Includes index.
    1. Taylor, Hannis, 1851–1922.   2. Politicians—
United States—Biography.   3. United States—Politics
and government—1865–1933.   4. United States—Foreign
relations—1865–1921.
E664.T17M3   329'.0092'4   [B]   77-17124
ISBN 0-8173-5114-0

Contents

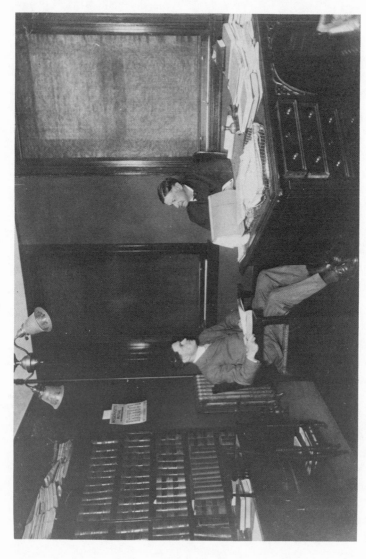

Hannis Taylor and his son, Hannis Joseph, in their Maryland Building law office, Washington, D.C., 1915

Preface

DURING THE LATE nineteenth and early twentieth centuries, American life took on contradictions that were later to surface with considerable poignancy. While many publicists and politicians foresaw an America of harmony and great opportunity, they also clung tenaciously to such doctrines as Anglo-Saxon racial superiority and the righteousness of liberal capitalism—notions that worked to defeat the progress they espoused. Here is a study of one of those persons, Hannis Taylor.

For a number of reasons Taylor's life is uniquely useful for the historian interested in the paradoxes of American life at the turn of the century. Unlike many others of the era who have been examined through biography, Taylor pursued the multifaceted career of practicing attorney, constitutional historian, journalist, diplomat, and ever-aspiring politician. Hence he had occasion to write and speak on almost every intellectual and popular issue of the period. His record serves as a microcosm of many of the contradictions spanning American thought during that time. Further, Taylor was a Southerner. Before moving to Washington, D.C. in 1902, Taylor had grown up in a North Carolina torn by the Civil War and had taken an active role in Alabama affairs during the three decades following Reconstruction. His life shows how a proponent of the New South creed could move easily to advocate the nationalistic foreign and domestic policies often associated with Theodore Roosevelt. Finally, from a humanistic standpoint Taylor's life permits a study in human strivings for achievement. American historiography gravitates to the successful; here is an account of a more common stereotype, the man who worked relentlessly at becoming a noted American by supporting popular causes and who failed tragically.

Hannis Taylor's papers have been sought for by several individuals, including the late J. G. deRoulac Hamilton of the University of North Carolina, but none succeeded in drawing them together as a collection. Thus my job was difficult. I had to ferret out his correspondence and papers from virtually every type of source that a researcher can work—from federal archives and well-cataloged personal manuscript collections to little-used local government manuscripts and unpublished memoirs. I actually found Hannis Taylor letters in attics and hall closets, a thrill which all historians should experience. So although researching and writing this book was at

times a confounding thing, it provided me with a decade of reward
and excitement.

Many individuals helped me locate materials. The staff of the
Southern Historical Collection, at the University of North Carolina,
provided their usual expert and cordial assistance. Numerous long-
time residents of Alabama and North Carolina were particularly
accommodating, too. They include Elizabeth Moore, Stephens and
Velma Croom, the late Palmer Pillans, the late Helen Taylor Abbot,
Regina Rapier Marston, David Mathews, Sr., Caldwell Delaney,
Milo B. Howard, Jr., Virginia K. Jones, Selinda Taylor Bewley, and
Gossett and Marian Taylor McRae. Still, Mary Lillie Taylor Hunt of
Boston—recently deceased, daughter of Hannis Taylor—served as
the most vital source of personal information and, indeed, an exceed-
ingly charming one.

There are also people who saw me through the writing of this book
in both personal and scholarly ways. I received strong encouragement
from Alice Atkins Mercer, Joe E. T. Buchanan, Ralph M. Tanner,
John F. Ramsey, Charles G. Summersell, Jack D. L. Holmes, J. Chal
Vinson, Melvin Herndon, Monseignor Oscar Lipscomb, David E.
Harrell, Jr., Ralph G. Holberg, Jr., B. G. Minisman, Jr., Lee M.
Shook, and Louis E. Braswell. I benefited greatly, too, from the
criticism and support offered by Numan V. Bartley, Jim Cobb, Tom
Dyer, Hardy Jackson, Clarence Mohr, Dick Clow, Jim Kitterman,
Richard Eubanks, and Willard Gatewood. Exercising skill and abiding patience, William F. Holmes of The University of Georgia
guided me through the organization and early drafting of the
manuscript. To Will, the major professor in the fullest sense of the
term, I am forever indebted. Paige, my wife, gave me her love, which
includes her striking sensitivity for people and history and words:
while she played a lively role in the reconceptualization of certain
critical parts of the book and in so doing added immeasurably to my
understanding of the social implications of America's past, what is
more important is that she, with Lanier, revitalized my sensitivity
toward the general condition of humanity. My parents, Dorothy and
Richebourg Gaillard McWilliams, were always there with encouragement and, out of their full experience as scholars, also made
valuable suggestions that directed me to materials in possession of the
people of Mobile. Semiannual conversations with Howell Raines and

Bill Cornwell kept me working. Jeanette Teal, Brenda Herron, Laura Parker, Debra Gorman, and Deborah Schuman exhibited an inspirational patience in typing the manuscript, over and over. Finally, The University of Alabama in Birmingham provided University College Faculty Research Grants during 1974–75 and 1975–76 which were essential to my research on the foreign affairs aspects of Hannis Taylor's career. To the University—to Dean Samuel B. Barker, to Dean George E. Passey, and especially to Professor Virginia Van der Veer Hamilton—I remain most grateful.

Grayton Beach, Florida   TENNANT S. MCWILLIAMS
May 1976

I

Carolina Youth

ON A HOT AUGUST afternoon in 1910 the Honorable Hannis Taylor of Washington, D.C. stood on the Academy Green in New Bern, North Carolina. Keynote figure in the town's bicentennial celebration, Taylor eloquently recalled his youth in this small coastal community. The Civil War was one of his central themes:

> I stand before you today as humble eye-witness to the beginning and the end of that dreadful Civil War.... If I could paint "on a ten league canvas with brushes of a comet's hair" the pictures which I saw in my youth, I could not convey to the minds of you younger men and women any adequate conception of the horrors of the Civil War.[1]

He emphasized the brutality of the war, not its gallantry. Further, Taylor never lamented the Confederate loss. Rather, he extolled the Union victory for he believed that secession was "a dangerous and entirely illogical heresy." He was proud that the United States remained, after all, "an indestructable union."[2]

Although he wrote critically of the Confederate cause, Taylor could trace his lineage deep into the South's history. His father, Richard Nixon Taylor, was the oldest son of William and Mary Hannis Taylor, who emigrated from Paisley, Scotland, to the North Carolina Sound area in 1810.[3] Richard, born in 1820, joined his father in a naval stores operation at New Bern.[4] The business did not do well, and following the death of his father in 1837, Richard concentrated his efforts on the brokerage of pine lumber. This venture met with great success.[5] In 1847 he was prosperous enough to court and marry Susan Stevenson,[6] whose ancestors were among the original proprietors in North Carolina and whose father was director of a highly successful shipping business.[7]

In the early years of their marriage Richard and Susan Taylor were happy. Richard's business continued to expand along with increased demands for pine lumber in the area, and by 1850 the enterprise had provided him with sufficient capital to purchase a general merchan-

1

dise store, several small farms, and a half-dozen slaves.[8] In their comfortable New Bern home on the north side of Broad Street, later to be known as the Eubanks House, the Taylors brought up a large family.[9] On September 12, 1851, their first-born arrived. He was named Hannis after Richard's mother.[10] Over the next seventeen years the Taylors had eight other children, two of whom died in infancy.[11] Providing for such a large family proved a great burden for the father, and in 1855, following reverses in the Tidewater pine industry, he was forced to declare bankruptcy. As a businessman he had shown himself to be inflexible and without foresight. Defeated, Richard had no strong desire to attempt a new financial start. The Stevenson family lent him money to establish another mercantile business, but the small store functioned for only two months.[12] In short, the Taylor family had fallen into economic difficulties by the time the oldest son, Hannis, reached four years of age. As an adult Hannis would strive for financial security, never forgetting the material want of his youth and the cause for that want, his father's failure in business.

Despite his father's inability in business, young Hannis enjoyed the stabilizing influence of a mother who placed a high value on social ability and education. Hannis's education easily could have been slighted with the family in such straits, but Mrs. Taylor would not allow it. With funds obtained from her father she enrolled Hannis in New Bern Academy, a private school offering instruction in mathematics, reading, and Latin.[13] Hannis met his mother's expectations and proved to be an able student, making particularly high marks in Latin.[14]

Mrs. Taylor viewed religious education as being as important as academic achievement. To the devotional lessons her son received at the Academy she added her own daily preaching on Biblical history and Baptist doctrine. Hannis enjoyed the instruction in ancient history, but despite an otherwise total dedication to his mother, he never became enthusiastic about the strict Protestant dogma she offered. The boy found such religion unnecessarily harsh, denying many of the frivolities of youth.[15] In later life he would react even more strongly against Protestant fundamentalism.

Hannis was ten when the Civil War began. The family remained in New Bern less than a year after North Carolina seceded, but this period was long enough for Hannis to receive indelible impressions of war around his home. As an adult he would recall the excitement with which he observed the first drills and target practice on the Academy Green. He would remember his fright as he witnessed the New Bern dead brought home from futile attempts at defending the outer Sound area.[16] In March 1862 Hannis, like hundreds of other children, fled inland with his family as General Ambrose E. Burnside led the Union assault on New Bern.[17] His family settled in Chapel Hill, and there lived through the remainder of the war far removed from the centers of battle. Yet, Hannis had some contact with the war. In April 1865 he witnessed the surrender of General Joe Johnston's Army of the Tennessee and shortly thereafter spent several days burying soldiers who died at the Raleigh military hospital.[18] Having seen the horror of war, he would not be able to glorify it in later years.

During the Civil War Richard Taylor helped manage a small textile mill near Chapel Hill and for two years after the war performed similar duties in the Raleigh area.[19] Whatever meager income such employment provided, much of it went to Hannis's education. Mrs. Taylor was determined that, regardless of war, her oldest son should receive a relatively uninterrupted education, one that would prepare him for college. Thus she was pleased to place Hannis under the tutelage of Cornelia Phillips Spencer, who spearheaded the reopening of the University of North Carolina after the Civil War.[20]

Along with four other boys, Hannis studied in Mrs. Spencer's home during 1863 and 1864. The tutor found her New Bern student to be bright but often uninterested. "He is smart enough to do very well," she observed with exasperation, "if he will only try!"[21] Mrs. Spencer was a devout Presbyterian whose constant moralizing partly accounted for Hannis's weak performance while under her supervision. Her lessons on literature and history were inseparable from her preachings on righteousness. In rejecting his tutor's strait-laced religion, young Taylor therefore appeared uninterested in the academic content of her instruction.[22] Furthermore, during the time he studied with Mrs. Spencer, Hannis lost his left eye in a hunting accident and that loss, too, in some measure accounted for his weak performance in school.[23] Yet this period of academic discouragement lasted less than a year. Since partial blindness eliminated him from many fast-moving outdoor activities, Hannis became an insatiable reader. By the time he left Mrs. Spencer's tutelage in 1864 he was reading every assignment enthusiastically and, on his own, was studying Greek and classical literature.[24]

Susan Taylor must have been encouraged by her son's scholarly achievements, even if he showed no interest in religion. In the last year of the war Hannis went on to D. C. Bingham's day school and several months later transferred to "the excellent classical school" of Dr. Alexander Wilson. Finally, when the family moved to Raleigh in early 1866, Hannis attended Lovejoy's School, where he remained through the spring of 1867 preparing for admission to college.[25]

In July 1867, at age seventeen, Hannis Taylor entered the University of North Carolina as part of a freshman class of twelve.[26] With disappointment he registered as a "partial course student," one who did not intend to graduate. He realized that because he could not depend on his father to keep the Raleigh job, he should not expect funds for more than one year of study. Yet, when this six-foot youth with olive complexion and coarse black hair strode onto the campus, he faced the scene with anticipation. Not only was he well prepared for college and excited about learning, but also he felt at home on the University grounds and even knew several students from his earlier stay in Chapel Hill.[27]

Hannis made good use of his one year at the University. He enrolled in courses on the British Empire and English literature, showing a youthful interest in English culture that would develop into a personal philosophy of Anglo-Saxon superiority during the next two decades.[28] Young Taylor also devoted a great deal of time to the Philanthropic Society, a reading and debating club. Aggressive as a debater, he often argued on freedom of the press and other aspects of American constitutionalism. Taylor became so involved during debate hour, indeed, that he continued to argue in the club's study hall and frequently received fines as high as seventy-five cents for annoying those trying to read. He was an adamant sort.[29]

In the spring of 1868 Richard Taylor lost his job at the Raleigh mill and moved the family back to New Bern. Now without his father's meager support, Hannis withdrew from the University and joined the family on the coast.[30] Again borrowing from the Stevensons, Richard Taylor leased a small mercantile store; but whatever profits this business provided, Hannis knew his father too well to expect him to give the family consistent support.[31] To supplement the family income, therefore, he went to work as a clerk in the law office of a prominent New Bern attorney, John N. Washington.[32]

Washington strongly influenced young Taylor. The attorney encouraged his clerk to read law and to take part in discussions that developed in the office. More important, in Washington's career Taylor saw a life which he not only respected but also actually wanted for himself. Washington had taken a law degree at Yale University, then returned to New Bern to establish himself as a scholarly attorney and a person of strong civic interest. He also was a Catholic who refused to accept social restraints often placed on Catholics in such strongly Protestant areas. Finally, Washington traveled extensively in Europe and enjoyed continental tastes in literature, food, and wine. Taylor viewed this attorney as a Southerner who had overcome much of the provincialism normally associated with the South. Such a worldly image greatly appealed to young Taylor, who later would become a scholarly attorney, a defender of religious freedom, and a man of sophisticated tastes and manners.[33]

After working as a law clerk for seven months, Taylor experienced a series of sudden shocks. John Washington died unexpectedly in February 1869.[34] The next month Richard Taylor's store failed, and Mrs. Taylor and one of the children, five-year-old Hannah, contracted tuberculosis. The Stevensons attempted to provide medical care for the family, but in June, Hannah died. When a physician advised Mrs. Taylor that she too would die if she did not move to another climate, she and the rest of the family made ready to leave behind the turbulence and tragedy of their lives in North Carolina.[35]

In July 1869 the Taylors moved to Point Clear, Alabama, a small town on the eastern shore of Mobile Bay where the climate was warmer and slightly drier than in New Bern. Richard went to work in a turpentine factory owned by his wife's brother-in-law, Theodore J. Jones, while Hannis tried to contribute to the family income by practicing law.[36] But the Taylors could not escape misfortune. On December 2, 1870, Susan died of tuberculosis, and two months later Richard lost his job. Then Hannis took his father, sister, and four brothers down to the mail boat and crossed over the bay to Mobile. At age twenty he became head of a large family.[37]

Hannis Taylor had experienced considerable instability as a youth in North Carolina. War interrupted his childhood, forcing the Taylor family to move three times in a six-year period and leaving Hannis with shocking impressions of violence. Hannis's father, moreover, offered the family no financial security. This economic distress was especially disappointing for Hannis because it prohibited him from continuing at the University of North Carolina. Then there were personal tragedies—Hannis's loss of an eye, his mother's death as well as the deaths of a brother and two sisters.

Still, young Taylor entered Mobile far from defeated. Mrs. Taylor and her parents had provided Hannis with basic education and social training. So, while he felt frustrated at not graduating from college, Hannis at least had the benefit of one year at Chapel Hill during a period when most young men of his age did not complete a secondary education. In late youth Hannis also profited from clerking with John Washington. Through this lawyer Hannis came into contact with a worldly and intellectual way of life which he determined to make his own. Thus, although Hannis Taylor encountered many problems in childhood, he still received more advantages than many who grew up during the Civil War. He arrived in Mobile with a purpose—to support the family and to build a career—and he possessed the social and intellectual abilities to do so.

II   Mobilian

WHEN HANNIS TAYLOR and his family entered Mobile in March 1871, they encountered a town of 30,000 people seething with resentment and distrust. Alabama had been readmitted to the Union in June 1868, but Republicans, some of whom were black, retained power in city and state politics.[1] "A self-assertion of the whites" provided the only chance for the future, declared the Democratic Mobile *Register*.[2] Responding to this call the Knights of the White Camellia intimidated Republican voters of both races in an attempt to return Democrats to municipal and state offices.[3] With the same purpose Democrats of Mobile supported their fellow citizen, Thomas H. Herndon, in the gubernatorial election of 1872. Although a Republican won that contest, many Democrats obtained seats in the state legislature. Two years later Democrats ousted Republican officeholders across the state, and most white citizens of Mobile felt gratified over the accompanying changes in their city government.[4]

By 1878 Hannis Taylor would become active in these and other political affairs of Mobile. Before he could take a role in public life, however, Taylor had to establish his family and develop a profession. Experience gained through work with John Washington enabled Hannis to secure a position as clerk in the law firm of James Bond and Decatur C. Anderson.[5] Providing for the family proved quite difficult for Hannis; a law clerk's salary did not go far in supporting seven people, four of whom were growing boys. Anderson assisted by giving Hannis salary advances, which the budding attorney used to lease a small house on Springhill Avenue. Hannis's spinster aunt, Elizabeth Taylor, also helped when she came from New Bern to live with the family. "Miss Betsy," as the family called her, brought efficiency to the Taylor household, but more important, she gave the younger children a mother's care.[6] Taylor was further encouraged in the spring of 1871 when his seventeen-year-old brother, Richard, found employment as an assistant in the office of a bond salesman and began bringing home a small but needed salary.[7] Yet what made Hannis most optimistic about the future was his father's decision to

7

make a new start. In August 1871, eight months after burying Susan, Richard Taylor married Louise McKenzie, a Talladega native whom he met while she visited relatives in Mobile.[8] Richard soon located a position as store manager at the Stonewall Cotton Mill in Mississippi and left Mobile with his bride and the four younger boys. When Mary, the remaining Taylor girl, decided to return to New Bern with Miss Betsy, Hannis stayed in Mobile—a town he had liked from the outset—and began to live free of family burdens.[9]

Taylor made good use of his new freedom. Resigning his position as clerk, he began to read law under the guidance of his former employer, D. C. Anderson. He borrowed money from his tutor and lived on a subsistence level.[10] After four months of study he passed the bar examination and in February 1872 was admitted to practice before the Alabama courts.[11] The young attorney went to work immediately. With Anderson's aid, Taylor obtained a temporary appointment as solicitor for sparsely populated Baldwin County. The job required him to make numerous trips across Mobile Bay, back through Point Clear near the burial site of his mother; but in return for the inconvenience of travel he received experience and a salary, both of which he desperately needed. Taylor even accumulated some savings after paying off his debt to D. C. Anderson.[12]

When Taylor found the opportunity to open a private law practice in Mobile, he could not resist it. Quitting his Baldwin County post after less than a year as acting-solicitor, he joined forces with another young attorney, Alfred Goldthwaite. In an upstairs office on St. Francis Street in the heart of Mobile, Taylor and Goldthwaite took on ordinary legal work—wills, deeds, undramatic civil suits.[13] Goldthwaite's uncle, former United States Supreme Court Justice John A. Campbell, sent a few important cases their way. In 1872, for example, Taylor and Goldthwaite represented the Bank of Kentucky in a real estate suit that went to the Alabama Supreme Court. The young attorneys lost the case, but they received a large fee and benefited by having argued against an experienced attorney, Thomas J. Semmes.[14]

Whatever funds Taylor had accumulated through two years of legal practice quickly were depleted early in 1874. Richard Taylor expanded operations of his store far beyond what the mill could support and, once again, lost his job. The boys came to live with Hannis, and

Richard's new wife returned to her family in Talladega. The father, "crushed in spirit," wandered first to St. Louis, then to New Bern, and finally back to Mobile to live with Hannis and his other children.[15] Young Richard shortly found employment in a barrel factory north of Mobile and moved out on his own. The rest of the family continued to depend on Hannis for support. He met this responsibility by purchasing a house on the outskirts of town where real estate costs were low. There he reestablished household operations and kept the family together.[16]

Despite his family obligations Taylor began to build a large circle of acquaintances. He made close friends within the elite families of Mobile, many of whom he met through John Rapier. As editor of the Mobile *Register* and an established attorney, Rapier had the opportunity to take Taylor to social gatherings and to introduce him to influential business leaders of the town.[17] Taylor further expanded his circle of friends when he began contributing articles on politics and law to the columns of the *Register*. Readers of the paper sought the company of this intelligent young writer, and they found him to be a person of "warmth and dignity," one very much in tune with the formal manners of the era. Indeed, he was chosen Felix, Emperor of Joy, for the Mardi Gras festivities of 1878.[18] In obtaining such an exalted social honor Hannis Taylor had accomplished no mean feat: he had climbed to the top of the Mobile social structure after living in this traditionalist town for only seven years.

In addition to Mobile's social qualities Taylor appreciated the city's open religious atmosphere in which many of the town's respected citizens, like John Rapier, practiced Catholicism free of discrimination.[19] Although he did not join a church in Mobile, Taylor developed lifelong relationships with Catholics of the city.[20] He felt especially close to Father Abram J. Ryan, a poet. While Ryan enjoyed little more than a regional reputation during the early 1870s, Taylor appreciated his work and even convinced the priest that he should publish his poems in a hard-bound volume.[21] When in 1876 Ryan was transferred to St. Mary's Church on the outskirts of the city, he settled directly across the road from Taylor's residence. The young attorney now began attending many of Ryan's services and frequently discussed religion with him. Taylor also observed the social context in which the priest worked.[22] In writing to his old Protestant tutor, Mrs.

Spencer, Taylor made these observations about Catholicism in Mobile:

> If you were to live where the [religious] forces were equally balanced, and could see the practical workings of good in both [Protestant and Catholic] systems . . . , mingle with the priesthoods of both divisions, and read Catholic literature in an equal proportion—you could say to yourself, "I have been misled as to the real nature of the [Catholic] church." The accounts of it in Protestant literature are neither fair nor true.[23]

The resistance to Protestant fundamentalism which Taylor displayed as a youth now began to develop into a conscious attraction to Catholicism.

Taylor also married into a prominent Catholic family. One Sunday afternoon in February 1877 Taylor walked across the road to visit with Father Ryan. Late that day the priest introduced Hannis to one of his parishioners, Leonora LeBaron. At nineteen the young lady was quite attractive; she had fair skin, deep brown eyes, black hair and was a slender five feet, seven inches tall.[24] Besides her beauty Hannis found other attractive qualities in Leonora. Her parents were William and Elizabeth LeBaron, who had large tracts of real estate in downtown Mobile and traced their ancestors far back into the French and Spanish culture that once flourished along the Gulf coast. Primarily because of this lineage William LeBaron simultaneously held the posts of Spanish and French consul at Mobile.[25] Moreover, the LeBarons had sent their daughter to the demanding Sacred Heart School in Baton Rouge, Louisiana, where she mastered such subjects as Spanish and French, besides furthering her religious education.[26] In short, Leonora LeBaron showed qualities that Hannis had long admired. Not only did she possess beauty and an established family background, but also she was well educated, sophisticated, and Catholic.

After a short courtship Hannis and Leonora married on May 8, 1878.[27] Settling into a Spring Hill residence, the young couple welcomed Hannis's father into their household. With them he spent the last six years of his life. By the time he died in 1884, the three other Taylor boys—George, William, and Jim—had moved out on their own as young Richard had done earlier.[28] The income which Hannis brought home from the expanding law firm, accordingly, enabled the Taylors to live quite comfortably. They enjoyed an active social life, and Hannis began to assume a role in the civic affairs of Mobile.

Taylor first gained recognition as a civic-minded Mobilian when, in 1878, he stepped forward to solve the city's debt predicament. Mobile Reconstruction debts totaled $500,000; because of continuing effects of the Panic of 1873, the city could not pay the interest on this sum, much less the principal.[29] With little knowledge of municipal finance, Taylor argued that, while the city should eliminate all nonessential services, no amount of retrenchment could ease Mobile's debt burden. Taylor suggested in addition to retrenchment a repeal of the Mobile city charter. Such action would dissolve the debtor city and thereby render the debts unenforceable. Under a new charter another city government might assume only that portion of the old debt it could finance. Taylor admitted that such a plan bordered on fiscal irresponsibility: if the city reneged on its debts, it might experience difficulty in obtaining credit in the future. But this objection to readjustment should be turned aside, he argued, because constitutional theory as well as legal precedent vouched for the fact that a city's charter could be revoked by the state legislature. Taylor then cited in great detail the theory and cases that substantiated his line of reasoning.[30]

At a public meeting held on the evening of December 6, 1878, Taylor worked with the city's Joint Committee on Laws and Ordinances to plan intricacies of the reform. With approval of the attending citizens, the Committee decided that a new three-member executive commission would determine what portions of the old debt should be assumed under the new charter.[31] Later a group of Mobile's leading citizens signed a petition endorsing Taylor's plan.[32] Finally, on February 11, 1879, the Alabama state legislature enacted the reform into law, and shortly thereafter the "City of Mobile" became the "Port of Mobile" according to the design of Hannis Taylor.[33]

In 1886 Mobile returned to the mayoral form of government, finding a commission too clumsy when quick decisions were needed.[34] Still, Hannis Taylor remained proud of his contribution to the city. In 1880 Mobile's delegation to the state legislature honored Taylor for these efforts by recommending him for an appointment to

the Alabama Supreme Court. Taylor lacked sufficient political leverage to obtain the position, but he felt encouraged even to have been
considered for such an appointment at age twenty-nine. Taylor had
sampled life in the public eye and liked it.[35]

With increased confidence and ambition Taylor expanded his law
practice, though he often worked alone after 1878 when Alfred
Goldthwaite moved to New Orleans.[36] Taylor became known as an
attorney who would doggedly pursue a case to the court of highest
level. Appearing some twenty-five times before the Alabama Supreme Court between 1880 and 1893, he represented such well-
paying clients as the Union National Bank of Mobile, the Mobile
Register Company, and that journal's editor, John Rapier. He claimed
victory in half of these cases.[37] Before the United States Supreme
Court Taylor also worked actively but often without success. Admitted to the Supreme Court Bar in 1885 under the sponsorship of
Senator John Tyler Morgan, Taylor argued a case before a year had
elapsed.[38] Representing the new Port of Mobile, he contended that
the new city was not obligated to honor certain bonds issued by the
old City of Mobile. Despite his intimate involvement with the facts
giving rise to the case, Taylor failed to convince the court that the city
government bore no responsibility.[39]

Taylor remained undaunted by this defeat as well as by numerous
other losses before Alabama courts. He had cultivated a poise, an
ability to speak, and an air of intellectualism which he felt people
respected.[40] To a degree he had cause for such confidence. Although
he failed to capture an appointment as a federal judge during Grover
Cleveland's first administration,[41] he began to receive numerous honors within Alabama. In 1883 he served as a vice-president for the
Alabama Bar Association.[42] Six years later he completed the first
volume of *Origin and Growth of the English Constitution* on which he had
worked for ten years. Recognizing this scholarly achievement, the
Alabama Bar immediately placed Taylor on its Committee for Jurisprudence and Law Reform, and two years later, in 1891, elected him
its president. When Taylor delivered the opening address at the 1891
meeting of the Bar, held in the luxurious Grand Hotel at Point Clear,
he enjoyed a considerable feeling of pride. Since moving from Point
Clear twenty years earlier he had advanced to the top of one of the
most respected professions in the state.[43]

The same year that Taylor achieved such professional prominence, he also experienced bitter defeat when serving as defense counsel in *Ex parte Rapier*.[44] That case concerned the limits of federal police power. In 1890 the United States Congress enacted a law prohibiting the advertisement of lotteries through the mails.[45] Because this law barred from the mails all newspapers that carried such advertisements, the *Register*'s editor John Rapier viewed the statute as a distinct encroachment on freedom of the press. To test the law Rapier printed an advertisement for the Louisiana State Lottery and mailed the issue at the United States Post Office at Mobile. When he received the expected indictment, he hired Taylor to challenge the law before the United States Supreme Court.[46] Accordingly, in November 1891, Taylor appeared before the court and attempted to show how the antilottery statute violated constitutional guarantees for press freedom. Employing his vast knowledge of English constitutional development, Taylor first discussed safeguards for press freedom engrained in English common law and demonstrated how these principles were incorporated into the United States Bill of Rights. He also cited cases that served as precedents for the inviolability of press freedom. That basic right, Taylor concluded, could not be sacrificed for the sake of federal lottery regulation.[47]

Attorneys for the government viewed Taylor's argument as "very edifying . . . [but] quite irrelevant." In less caustic terms, Chief Justice Melvin W. Fuller, writing for the court, agreed: Taylor had failed to comprehend the high priority that had to be placed on national regulation of such social evils as lotteries.[48] If prominent attorneys and journalists across the country found Taylor's defense of press freedom to be "unanswerable,"[49] such national recognition was not enough to salve Taylor's wounded pride. He took the court's opinion as a personal affront. Through an article in the *North American Review*, he would later lash out at all nine justices, proclaiming that the rejection of his argument represented "a judge-made proviso," one which "prostrated at a blow the bulwark which the fathers fancied they had built between Congressional tyranny and freedom of opinion." Futilely, he predicted that "this heresy will be repudiated."[50] Although Hannis Taylor would eventually become a strong supporter of the federal police power advocated by Theodore Roosevelt, he never forgave the court for its decision in *Ex parte Rapier*.[51]

Following presentation of the Rapier case Taylor headed back to Mobile. If life there offered fewer professional opportunities than he encountered in the nation's capital, in Mobile the winters were warmer, life moved at a slower pace, and his large family occupied a position of social prominence. Time would come when Taylor would not think so kindly of Alabama. But in November 1892 he was pleased to be returning to the balmy port town and to his household.[52]

The Taylors' family was large. Their first child, Charles, was born in their second year of marriage and in 1884 Mary Lillie arrived. Over the the next six years the Taylors had three more children: Hannah, Hannis Joseph, and Alfred.[53] In 1888 Taylor placed his family in a spacious home in Dauphin Street. Proud of his ability to provide, he told the children that he had purchased the home because of the huge oak trees that surrounded it—excellent swings could be hung from these trees.[54] Taylor ruled his home with customary nineteenth-century formality. He required the children to keep clean and neatly dressed even after school, and he set a high standard for them by always remaining in coat and tie until bedtime. He continually in-structed the children on speaking correctly. As they developed read-ing ability, he encouraged them to devote their free time to classical literature, as he had in his youth.[55] Taylor made abundantly clear his reverence for great books on the afternoon that Mary Lillie's pet goat slipped into the house, located the study, and dared to eat the major portion of Taylor's favorite copy of *The Inferno*. Taylor never said a word about the destroyed book, but after that day the children never saw the goat again.[56] Although Taylor was a demanding father, his children still felt very close to him and valued his presence. Taylor knew of their affection and often spent hours with them in the eve-ning. When work kept him at the law office until late, he conscien-tiously visited with them when he returned home, occasionally giving each a snack of hot oyster loaf brought from downtown.[57]

The serious yet warm personality which Taylor showed at home he also exhibited to friends in the community. As he grew older the popularity he enjoyed as a young Mobilian continued to increase.[58] In the nineties he often dined at the Athelstan Club, an elite men's club near his office. There he visited with such fellow civic leaders as Peter Alba, Stephens Croom, and Ed Russell.[59] These gentlemen respected Taylor for his desire, if not ability, to consume great quantities of broiled pompano. He also amazed friends by determining the exact origin of a wine according to its taste. His doctor advised him to limit such epicurean activities in order to avoid recurring seizures of gout, but Taylor had worked hard for such pleasures and would not be denied—despite the pain of gout.[60]

As a mature citizen of Mobile, Taylor received greatest respect for his public philosophy and scholarly endeavors.[61] In 1878 he had established himself as a proponent for a new Mobile by offering a solution to the city's debt problem. Yet, he became known as more than a Mobilian. Taylor developed an identity as an advocate of the New South, espousing much of the message preached by Henry W. Grady and other Southern editors. To move into a new era, these publicists asserted, Southerners must achieve sectional reconciliation with the North, racial harmony, industrial expansion, and agricultural diversification. Despite the contradiction, these Southerners also called for a glorification of the Old South—a "vital nexus" with the security of the past.[62]

Taylor advocated economic changes that complemented the New South creed. As a contributor to a multivolume history of the state, *The Memorial Record of Alabama*, Taylor in 1893 expressed the booster spirit used by many Southerners to encourage industry and commerce. He believed that the destruction of slavery freed the South from its near-total commitment to agriculture and provided the region with a chance to develop a more diversified economy. Furthermore, with the state's abundance of minerals Taylor believed that Alabama enjoyed great advantages over other Southern states. Not only did mining itself provide great profits, he explained, but also coal and iron served as essential ingredients for a booming steel industry.[63] As a Mobilian, Taylor also identified with shipbuilding. During 1888 he delivered speeches in Birmingham and Anniston, encouraging business leaders to support this industry. He urged Senator Morgan to make real the often proposed plans for establishing a naval shipyard at Mount Vernon above Mobile near the Alabama River. "If such a result can be accomplished," he wrote the senator, "it will be the most important fact which has occurred in the post bellum history of the state."[64] Taylor's enthusiasm proved futile. While Congress allocated funds for the deepening of Mobile harbor during the eighties and nineties, it refused to support naval shipbuilding in the state.[65]

At the same time that Taylor encouraged his fellow citizens to develop a diversified economy, he urged Southerners to strive for sectional reconciliation and national identification. Indeed, those reading Taylor's contribution to the *Memorial Record* found the Mobilian serving as the most optimistic of American patriots. He condemned Southern sectionalism, which had helped bring on the Civil War. America could not have become strong, he asserted, if the doctrine of nullification and the institution of slavery had been allowed to stand.[66] If the Civil War was violent, disruptive, and tragic, as Taylor remembered it to be, the conflict nevertheless brought great progress to the nation as a whole. Hence he concluded his assessment of the Southern past on notes of optimism and patriotism: "Heavy has been the price which has been paid for the peace we now enjoy, but the comfort is in the thought that it must be permanent and lasting. . . . All of the great causes which divided the nation have been forever eradicated."[67]

If Taylor explicitly showed a nationalistic attitude towards politics and economics in the South, he implicitly displayed a national identification through scholarly writing on the history of England. During the late nineteenth century intellectual racism served as a powerful element in American scholarship, and Taylor reflected this quality in writing *Origin and Growth of the English Constitution*.[68] He emphasized the theme that people of predominantly Teutonic origin, such as the Caucasians, had progressed further along the evolutionary scale than those of other heritages. The Caucasians in England and the United States served as prime examples of Teutonic superiority.[69]

Over a long period of time Taylor had developed this philosophy of Teutonic superiority. While studying at Chapel Hill he began reading in English and European history. After establishing his law practice he read more widely in those fields.[70] In the early eighties Taylor determined to study the evolution of American governmental practices as they had grown out of the English constitutional experience. He firmly believed that the Teutonic germ as it had been planted in England represented the origin of America's superior form of federalism. In explaining his objective to Herbert Baxter Adams, Taylor wrote:

> Until [the student] gains clear insight into the marvelous process of
> historical development which binds the little group of Teutonic states,

as [they were] originally established in Britain, to the group of English
states planted ten centuries later upon the Eastern coast of what is now
the United States, our constitutional history must ever remain a sealed
book to him. [71]

By 1885 Taylor was engrossed in writing. Two or three nights a
week he retired to his study after supper and worked until early
morning. Considering Taylor's devotion to his children as well as his
activity as an attorney, he displayed enormous energy in carrying out
such a project. [72] Encouragement from numerous individuals helped
to keep him working. Harvard historian John Fiske expressed disbe-
lief when he first heard that an unknown Southerner had undertaken
such a study. After corresponding with Taylor and reading portions
of the manuscript, nevertheless, Fiske praised Taylor and encouraged
him to publish the work as soon as possible. [73] Edward A. Freeman,
the noted English historian, echoed Fiske's enthusiasm. In 1887
Freeman spent three days with Taylor at St. Louis, helping him
delineate certain complicated forms of early Teutonic government. [74]
Herbert Baxter Adams supplied the most valuable aid: he read and
criticized selected portions of the manuscript, and in 1888 he submitted the unpublished work to his seminars at The Johns Hopkins
University and relayed to Taylor the students' criticisms. [75]

Through Fiske's influence Taylor contracted with Houghton
Mifflin to publish *Origin and Growth of the English Constitution*. In 1889
the first volume appeared and nine years later the second. [76] Southern
journals hailed Taylor's scholarship as evidence of an intellectual
renaissance in their region. National journals also gave Taylor favorable reviews, as did such British journals as London's *Pall Mall
Gazette*. The Earl of Meath even cited Taylor's work as evidence of
increasing Anglo-American unity. By writing with such respect for
the English culture, the Earl claimed, Taylor had helped ensure "the
future supremacy of the Anglo-Saxon race." [77] William A. Dunning,
Columbia University historian, contended that the study reflected
too little research in primary materials—a criticism that also would be
aimed at Taylor's later writings. [78] Despite this drawback, Taylor's
racial views proved popular and profitable. At least fourteen prominent law schools adopted *Origin and Growth of the English Constitution*,
including those of Harvard and Georgetown universities. [79]

Taylor gained the reputation of an enlightened Southerner principally because of his contribution as a legal historian. Even so, his reputation was not limited to political and academic circles. As a member of the Executive Board of the Mobile Medical College, Taylor became a strong supporter of Mobile physicians and the improved health conditions toward which they worked. He made this quite clear by allowing Mobile doctors to perform the port city's first appendectomy on his youngest daughter, Hannah. Although many waiting outside the infirmary viewed the occasion as no less exciting than a hanging, Hannis's faith in Mobile medicine was borne out when surgeons reported a total success.[80] More important, in 1890 Taylor drafted a $20,000 state appropriation bill to expand facilities at the Medical College. The fund would be used to purchase more laboratory equipment, to increase faculty salaries, and to provide free treatment for poor people of the state. When the bill came before the legislature in 1891, Taylor appeared before a joint session and spoke in favor of the proposal.[81] His efforts failed. Retrenchment took its toll when the politicians allotted only $10,000 for the Medical College.[82] Although Taylor was disappointed over the actions of the legislature, in other matters he too served the interests of conservative politics.

Indeed, Taylor became known as much for his conservatism as for his advocacy of change and thereby exemplified the contradictions of the New South creed. Although Taylor refused to glorify the Civil War, he identified with social and political values of the Old South and openly criticized intrusions upon that old order. Taylor's social drive as well as his marriage into the LeBaron family brought him quick acceptance by the elite of Mobile. His circle of friends and the honors he received at Mardi Gras also demonstrated this popularity.[83] Further, Taylor showed his identification with the old order by writing Alabama history that reflected many of the themes soon to be popularized by William A. Dunning.[84] Taylor charged that Congressional Reconstruction upset the social structure of the Old South, bringing on "an epoch of violence and crime" in the region. "The conqueror at once put the knife to the bottom of the wound," he wrote, and "subjected the conquered to the full force of his evolutionary theory."[85] Through the enactment of black codes the South tried to solve the problem of disorganized labor precipitated by emancipation, Taylor declared, but the Republican party had foiled those efforts by sending to the South the "disreputable" agents of the Freedmen's Bureau. He blamed the agents for all the racial tensions in the post-Reconstruction South. "By the evil influences of these agents . . . , the minds of the newly emancipated slaves were poisoned with all kinds of impossible expectations. . . . [The agents] were official organizers of crime and discontent." Despite the Republicans' efforts to disrupt the South's social stability, Taylor believed that whites were establishing a satisfactory racial order through the enactment of Jim Crow laws.[86]

Taylor wrote just as critically of post-Reconstruction Republican politics as he did of that party's Reconstruction policies. When in 1879 Republicans sought to extend the use of federal troops in supervising Southern elections, Taylor not only used the columns of the *Register* to villify the Republican party in general but also characterized President Rutherford B. Hayes as "a weak person" easily controlled by partisan pressures.[87] A decade later he lashed out at another noted Republican, House Speaker Thomas B. Reed. In the Mobilian's view, Reed always worked against Democratic bills, the only type of legislation that might benefit the South.[88]

If Taylor believed that the Democratic party alone served the interests of the South, he also adhered to the Southerners' traditional belief in states' rights. He could not even accept the Blair Education Bill.[89] Despite educational monies the bill would send to the South, he viewed federal financing of public education as an encroachment upon the state's realm of responsibility.[90] Taylor felt relieved when the Blair Bill met defeat. He congratulated Senator Morgan for his opposition to the proposal, confiding to the Senator that he felt "humiliated by the [affirmative] position taken by the majority of southern senators on the question."[91]

In Mobile, accordingly, Taylor emerged as a man caught up in paradox. He stood for readjustment, social welfare legislation, and religious freedom yet supported the conservative social and political establishment of the South. He believed that the abolition of slavery was economically progressive; yet he lived by the values of white supremacy. He called for national political allegiance yet encouraged the politics of sectionalism. As a Mobilian, Hannis Taylor lived in a dilemma common to many Southerners. He wanted the South to break away from its provincial past and to live according to national standards. Still, he could not accept the changes in his society that served as the means to Southern advancement. His philosophy exemplified the contradictions of the New South creed— contradictions that defeated efforts to change the South during the late nineteenth century and most of the twentieth century.

In Mobile Taylor did overcome many of the deficiencies of his youth. With pride he could point to his spacious home, to his bright and charming wife, and to five well-mannered and intelligent children. He could feel at least partially satisfied with his profession; even if he lost some important cases, his law practice provided the family with solid support. Finally, he could walk down Government Street confident that he had a reputation as a man of intellectual, social, and civic importance.

III   Diplomat
                      in Spain

HANNIS TAYLOR ENJOYED the respect of many attorneys and politicians of Alabama, as well as the esteem of noted historians, but his increasing ambition drove him to pursue a role in public life. In 1891 he tried and failed to win an appointment as state Supreme Court justice.[1] The following year he attempted, unsuccessfully, to capture an appointment as United States counsel at the Bering Sea Tribunal.[2] Finally, in 1893 Taylor obtained a public office. He became United States minister to Spain in Grover Cleveland's second administration. Taylor had no credentials for service as a diplomat; he could not even read Spanish, much less converse in it. He was known as an "orthodox Democrat," however, at a time when diplomatic appointments often were awarded on the basis of patronage. Thus when Cleveland determined to award the Madrid post to a Southerner noted for having withstood the bolt to Populism, he took the advice of Alabama's Democratic hierarchy and gave the appointment to Taylor.[3]

On the morning of April 15, 1893, Taylor received official communication of his appointment. Secretary of State Walter Quinton Gresham notified Taylor that he would serve as Envoy Extraordinaire and Minister Plenipotentiary with offices at Madrid. Taylor's initial excitement quickly faded. Although that title had a nice ring, he had hoped for the newly created top rank of ambassador with an annual salary of more than $12,000. After John Rapier discovered that the rank of minister was standard for the Madrid post, however, Taylor regained his exuberance and that same day took the oath of office from federal Judge Harry J. Toulmin. That night Hannis and Leonora began to make plans for the move. Because Taylor had no major cases in progress at the time, he dispensed with the law practice by arranging for other attorneys to manage the affairs of his retainer clients.[4]

One month later, accompanied by five children and an Irish nurse, they left Mobile and traveled to Washington, D.C., for a three-day stopover. Taylor met with President Cleveland and received the enlightening instructions, "Stay where we have sent you." On May

24 the Taylors departed from the capital, traveled to New York, and from there embarked on the month's voyage to Spain with brief stops at Southampton and Paris.[5] Since the new minister did not speak Spanish, it was with considerable difficulty that he and his family entered Madrid on June 20, 1893, and made their way to the American apartment, Ca de Sedaño 38. The following two weeks Taylor devoted to personal matters—getting oriented in the city, placing the girls in a convent school, and hiring a tutor for the boys.[6]

The Taylor family found Madrid fascinating. Shortly after arriving, Hannis felt obligated to take the family to a bullfight, Spain's national sport. Although the children enjoyed the excitement and color of the crowd, they became frightened when the bull met his gory death. Indeed, Hanna and Mary Lillie refused to return to the bullfights. When the rest of the family went to the arena, the girls attended matinees under their nurse's supervision. They took in the "racy" plays—an adventure which Hannis and Leonora never discovered. Still, Madrid had other attractions the children enjoyed more openly.[7] Birthday celebrations for royal youths always were gala affairs for the Taylor children. At one party each guest received a small dog as a favor. If Hannis had little appreciation for a pet goat, he had less appreciation for several puppies. When the dogs ignored discipline and continually nipped the minister on the ankles, Hannis gave them away, much to the children's sorrow. Other aspects of Madrid life Taylor believed to be more important for his children. He wanted them to meet important people. He introduced them to his new friends, such noted statesmen as Ambassador Henry Drummond Wolfe of Great Britain and Emilio Castelar of Spain. Furthermore, Taylor felt pleased about the children's increasing facility with Spanish. Indeed, Mary Lillie learned Spanish so well that for several months after returning to the United States she experienced difficulty speaking English.[8]

After helping the family adjust to a new life, Taylor finally presented his credentials to the Spanish queen on July 4, 1893, and opened the ministry.[9] He assumed his duties under difficult circumstances. The Spanish *Cortes* (Congress) remained under the influence of conservatives during most of the 1890s. With proud visions of retaining Spanish possessions in the western hemisphere, conservatives demonstrated extreme sensitivity to the expanding American influence. While a few liberals wanted to deal pragmatically with the United States, conservatives contrived every conceivable legal delay to stymie American relations with Cuba, something Taylor would erroneously perceive as Spanish "procrastination." This problem became particularly poignant regarding Cuban affairs. The *Cortes* balked when the second Cuban revolution began in 1895, and many Americans urged Spain to implement reforms on the island. Indeed, the *Cortes* delayed so very long in acting on the issue of Cuban reform that some Americans felt a Spanish-American war would serve as the only means to Cuban freedom. Even before the Cuban crisis, however, Taylor experienced several encounters with anti-American feeling in the Spanish government.[10]

Because of "procrastination" in the *Cortes*, for example, Taylor was forced to labor with what otherwise would have been a minor dispute, the Mora claim. That dispute had been a matter of contention since 1870, when Spanish authorities had confiscated the Cuban sugar plantations of Antonio Maximo Mora, a naturalized United States citizen. Some Spanish officials admitted to the illegality of the confiscation, but others in the *Cortes* intended to block payment of the $1,500,000 indemnity until the United States paid Spain debts originating in the Florida cession of 1819. Taylor had the assignment of collecting the Mora indemnity without meeting the Spanish claim.[11]

For four months following his arrival Taylor urged Spanish Foreign Minister Antonio Moret to renew discussions on the Mora claim. Fearing the antagonism of his conservative opposition in the *Cortes*, Moret simply ignored Taylor's notes.[12] Under additional pressure from the United States secretary of state, Taylor finally cornered Moret in late 1893. The ensuing conference produced no solution. Moret informed Taylor that the *Cortes* would not vote the indemnity until the Florida debt had been settled. In a calm tone Taylor replied that Spain's initial agreement to pay the indemnity included no such condition and that Washington frowned on Spain's continued "procrastination" in the affair. Admitting to Spanish fault, Moret suddenly appeared cooperative. He promised to sponsor a bill for payment, and Taylor concluded that the issue was settled.[13] Actually, the American minister had been duped. Taylor attended to other diplomatic business, recovered from a case of pneumonia, and

awaited passage of Moret's bill. Twelve months later the *Cortes* still
had not acted on the matter. In 1895 at Gresham's urgent insistence,
Taylor again requested payment of the claim. This time Moret replied that payment would be made "when the occasion arrives."
Taylor backed off and temporarily dropped the issue.[14]

When newly appointed Secretary of State Richard Olney questioned Taylor on his inactivity in the case, Taylor frustratedly reported that he needed more than "ordinary means" of diplomacy to
bypass Spanish politics. Taylor did not specify what other approach
was needed, and Olney did not ask. The new secretary of state
erroneously attributed the holdup to Taylor's inefficiency. Olney
personally took charge of the case. To his frustration, Olney's efforts
also became stifled by Spanish delay tactics, and not until Americans
increased their agitation over the Cuban revolution during the summer of 1895 did Spain finally appear ready to pay the indemnity in an
attempt to soothe anti-Spanish sentiment in the United States. Even
with that leverage Olney had to resort to exceptional means of diplomacy; in late August he obtained a decree from the queen to bring the
matter to a close. Taylor felt vindicated.[15]

Taylor's difficulty with Spanish politics appears more clearly in his
management of the Carolines claim. In 1890 three ministers of the
American Board of Protestant Missions worked among the natives
living on Ponape, one of many small islands in the Spanish-owned
Carolines group east of the Philippines. Certain Madrid officials had
sanctioned the Protestant activity in the Catholic domain. In late
1890, however, Spanish naval officers reacted to anti-American feeling in the *Cortes* by expelling the Protestants from Ponape and confis-
cating their buildings and supplies. The Spanish cabinet promised to
rectify this situation by relocating the missionaries and paying an
indemnity of $17,500.[16] When Taylor received the assignment of
actually obtaining that settlement, he nevertheless confronted a *Cortes*
determined to oppose any such concession to Americans.

After studying the case during August 1893, Taylor advised Secretary of State Walter Q. Gresham that conservatives in the Spanish
government would block final settlement of the Carolines claim unless
the State Department gave him authority to take some "firmer action"
than merely repeatedly requesting settlement according to customary
practice.[17] At first Gresham did not heed this warning. He instructed

his minister to use ordinary means in the affair. Taylor obeyed and made no headway.[18] In mid-April 1894 Taylor again urged the secretary of state to change tactics. Elaborating on his earlier remarks, Taylor wrote Gresham that "what the [Spanish cabinet] fears is the hostility of the extremists in the *Cortes* which will manifest itself the moment that permission is given here for the missionaries' return." Taylor believed that payment of the indemnity was agreeable to most of the Cabinet. Returning the missionaries, nonetheless, represented too great a political gamble for them, he reasoned. Thus Taylor recommended to Gresham that the requests be separated: first the American minister would attempt to obtain the indemnity; then at a later date—perhaps under changed political conditions—he would attempt to deal with restitution of the missionaries. Gresham agreed to that plan.[19]

In a more aggressive tone Taylor immediately pressured Moret for the full indemnity. During early May, Foreign Minister Moret again sought delays. He engaged Taylor in debate on what type of currency would be used if payment finally was agreed upon.[20] Finally, on June 5, 1894, Taylor called on Moret and presented the written statement that Madrid's continued foot-dragging would "severely damage" Spanish-American relations. The tone more than the content of the assertion shocked Moret. He capitulated and within three weeks had exerted enough political force to obtain the necessary appropriation of $17,500 in gold. Showing great national pride, Taylor informed Moret that an air of "pleasantness" now might be restored to Spanish-American relations.[21] Yet when he left Madrid, Taylor could not look upon the Carolines claim with total satisfaction. For the next two years he intermittently worked at restitution of the missionaries. He never succeeded. *Cortes* conservatives were too proud of the Spanish-Catholic domain to stop what was, in Taylor's view, "procrastination" on that portion of the agreement. Equally significant, increasing Spanish-American tensions in the Caribbean required that Taylor give less and less attention to affairs in the Pacific.[22]

Cubans revolted against Spanish authority in February 1895. Many citizens of the United States extended their sympathy to Cuba: some called for Cuban independence, some for Cuban autonomy, and some for simply a negotiated peace that would end the bloody civil war. When Americans began to send arms to the insurrectionists, Spain demonstrated extreme sensitivity to all ships of American registry sailing near Cuba.[23] Taylor's first dramatic encounter with this situation was his management of the *Alliança* affair.

During March 1895 a Spanish gunboat fired on the American mail ship *Alliança* as it sailed in international waters off the Cuban coast.[24] Upon instruction from Gresham, Taylor immediately protested the incident. The Spanish foreign minister blithely replied that Cuban authorities had not filed a report on such an episode. This excuse, plus a change in personnel at the Spanish Foreign Ministry, forestalled official consideration of the affair until April.[25] At that time, however, Taylor pursued the issue in polite but aggressive language. He declared that the United States "had never recognized and never will recognize any pretense or exercise of sovereignty on the part of Spain beyond a belt of half a league from the Cuban coast." Despite conservative opposition in the *Cortes*, some Spanish officials feared that the incident might encourage American intervention in Cuba and now admitted to Taylor that the attack had been unjustified. Taylor studied the draft of a note which Madrid intended to issue in formal apology and advised that the note was insufficient. Spain must make more emphatic its admission of error, Taylor asserted, and must offer more definite assurances against further actions of that sort. Spain followed Taylor's advice in sending a formal apology to Washington on April 18. In addition, when the Cuban report finally arrived and attested to the Spanish error, Taylor had the foreign minister write Washington that Spain bore no hard feelings toward "the great American republic" because of the unfortunate episode.[26]

As the Cuban revolution expanded during October 1895, President Cleveland, under pressure from Congress, instructed Taylor to sample Spanish reaction toward a proposed "impartial" American investigation of the Cuban problem. Inopportunely, Taylor was recuperating from rheumatism at LaGranja when his office received these important instructions.[27] Apprised of the plans, Taylor quickly returned to his post and called upon Premier Antonio Cánovas del Castillo. He presented the proposal in terms as cordial as possible. Premier Cánovas nevertheless rejected Cleveland's plan as meddling by a foreign power. Taylor agreed with Cánovas. While the American minister had been stern with Madrid in previous negotiations, in this case he advised Olney that the proposed investigation appeared too aggressive and would violate Spanish-American amity. Indeed, Taylor prepared an article for the *North American Review* in which he criticized the proposal and asserted that Spain would solve the Cuban problem without American interference. Cleveland "heartily concurred" with Taylor but nevertheless advised Taylor to withhold the article until after the Annual Message scheduled for December 2, 1895, when he would present a view similar to Taylor's. Then, in late December, Cleveland suggested, Taylor could release the article in affirmation of the address. Taylor agreed to this plan—at least temporarily.[28]

Although Taylor increased his favor with the Cleveland administration by withholding the article, he quickly negated that positive impression. The president called for American neutrality according to the agreed-upon plan.[29] Taylor, however, refused to publish the supporting article. In a month's time the American minister totally reassessed the question of American neutrality regarding Cuba. Developments in Spanish politics served as one cause for Taylor's change of view. Throughout November 1895 Taylor saw what he perceived to be increased inefficiency in the Spanish government. With liberals temporarily controlling the *Cortes* but conservatives now dominating the cabinet, the government became virtually paralyzed. Under these conditions, Taylor believed, Spain would never grant concessions to Cuba, and the revolution would continue until the United States intervened. Further, as 1895 came to a close, Taylor became more and more excited over pro-Cuban sentiment, which was mounting in the American Congress and American press. Valeriano Weyler, the Spanish general charged with quelling the insurrection, reportedly employed ruthless methods in corralling Cuban patriots. Regardless of their debatable authenticity, Taylor believed the atrocity stories on Weyler and viewed the Cubans' existence under his policies as a life of oppression and inhumanity. Furthermore, talk of American intervention to halt Weyler's activities excited Taylor's sense of nationalism; he viewed the United States as the guardian of the western hemisphere. When Henry Cabot Lodge visited Madrid in late 1895, Taylor jumped at the chance to explain his changed view on Cuba to the Republican senator whose expansionist sentiment and faith in the Anglo-Saxon he had so long admired. Lodge encouraged Taylor,

perhaps even with a promise to try to extend his Madrid appointment
for another four years should Republicans win the 1896 presidential
election. Whatever his political considerations, years later Taylor
reflected on his abrupt turnabout: "When the last outbreak in Cuba
fell upon my ears, I must confess I did not heed it as I should. But as
that cry deepened I soon came to understand its true and real significance."[30]

To rectify his earlier lack of attention to Cuban reform, therefore,
Taylor drafted another article during late November. That manuscript, in contrast to the one Cleveland approved, described the
inability of the Spanish government to solve the Cuban dilemma and
called for an end to American neutrality. In writing the article Taylor
displayed a total disregard for his official status in Madrid. Fortu-
nately, he sent a copy to Olney and Cleveland before releasing the
manuscript to the *North American Review*. Olney's reaction was what
Taylor should have expected. "In as much as [the article] criticizes a
long established policy of the United States," advised Olney, "it may
subject you to censure." If he were looking to a future appointment
under the Republicans, Taylor still valued his current job. As United
States relations with Spain became increasingly tense over Cuba,
furthermore, he was indeed gaining more and more prominence. So
Taylor abided by Olney's warning and withheld the controversial
manuscript. He would publish it later.[31]

While Taylor withheld public statements encouraging American
intervention in Cuba, he nevertheless accomplished little that improved Spanish-American relations during the remainder of his assignment. On one occasion Taylor personally produced a matter of
potential friction between the two countries. In February 1896 a
Spanish naval captain reportedly told a Madrid audience that he
found Americans "very materialistic [and] out for the dollar." When
Taylor heard this statement, he immediately protested. The State
Department in Washington refused to acknowledge Taylor's action as
official. The Spanish foreign minister, furthermore, found Taylor's
protest without any basis; the captain had made no such statement.
Fearing increased tensions of any sort with the United States, however, the Spanish Premier forced the captain to apologize just the
same, and Taylor felt vindicated.[32]

In the spring of 1896 Taylor again took advantage of Spain's desire to avoid friction with the United States. As Madrid struggled with rejecting Cleveland's new offer to mediate the Cuban problem, the *Competitor* affair developed. Cuban officials captured American filibusters on board the *Competitor* and with a summary court-martial sentenced them to death.[33] Responding to instructions, Taylor protested the treatment of the Americans. First, he forced the Spanish premier to suspend the men's sentences until a civil trial could determine their guilt or innocence. Then he influenced the pending civil proceedings by proclaiming the right to inspect all records of litigation. In short, this action meant that the United States would object to any trial that convicted the men. Under pressure of rejecting Cleveland's mediation offer, the premier acquiesced to Taylor's demands. Thus Taylor sent Olney the dramatic news that he had nullified all charges on the *Competitor* group by working through "confidential sources."[34]

Meanwhile, during the spring of 1896, journalists and politicians in the United States increased their demands for belligerency status for Cuba and the eventual independence of the island. In reaction to American aggressiveness the people of Madrid became quite hostile toward Minister Taylor and his family. Anti-American demonstrations occurred at bullfights and parks. Whereas the presence of the Taylors once had been considered essential for diplomatic social gatherings, many Spanish officials now treated the American couple like persona non grata. Even Taylor's own servants became hostile. On one occasion they actually served the minister's soup in a chamber pot. Taylor responded by placing armed guards around his apartment and by making arrangements to move operations to the German embassy if the guards encountered difficulty. He was not forced to make that move. Yet, tensions did increase, and Taylor became so concerned over the physical safety of his family that in June 1896 he sent them home to Mobile. To avoid further friction Taylor announced that his family had returned to the United States simply for a visit.[35] When unfounded rumors reported that the premier had asked Taylor himself to leave the country, however, the American minister began to execute his duties with overt pride. Later that summer he refused to travel the streets of Madrid without riding in the official

American carriage, which displayed golden eagles on each door. He continued to attend bullfights despite boos he received when he took his seat. He ordered all military personnel at the legation not to appear in public without full uniform.[36]

In such a strained atmosphere Taylor took on the most important role of his assignment. On August 7, 1896, the Spanish foreign minister secretly asked European diplomats to sign a protest against possible American intervention in Cuba. Although no one signed the protest at that time, the diplomats reacted favorably to the scheme. The plan was foiled, however, when Sir Henry Drummond Wolfe, British ambassador at Madrid, divulged it to an English journalist. The newspaperman, a Mr. Houghton, immediately approached Taylor for a reaction to the scheme. When Taylor heard of the plan he became enraged at such a clandestine threat to the United States. Using the excuse that Olney was away from Washington on vacation at the time, Taylor determined to advance himself by proceeding without instructions.[37]

To defeat the scheme Taylor caused the defection of its two most influential participants, the ambassadors of France and Great Britain. He viewed them as cautious men fearful of making important decisions. Approaching them "with a high tone of indignation," Taylor raged that the scheme represented a direct violation of the Monroe Doctrine and a breach of long-established friendships. His approach worked. They apologized and promised to do all that was possible to block completion of the plan. Wolfe, moreover, arranged for Taylor to discuss the matter with the Spanish foreign minister. In the ensuing conversation, Taylor posed as one loyal to Cleveland's Cuban policy. When the foreign minister admitted to the scheme, Taylor chastised him for ignoring Cleveland's repeated statements of American neutrality. In a reply to this rebuke the foreign minister explained that the upcoming presidential election in the United States would place a Republican in the White House, one who favored intervention. Perhaps an interventionist would be elected, Taylor replied, but not necessarily a Republican. Taylor declared that even if William Jennings Bryan, a Democrat, became the next president, and Senator John Tyler Morgan the new secretary of state, Madrid should make sufficient concessions to solve the Cuban crisis before Cleveland left office, for Bryan and Morgan, like McKinley, advocated American

intervention in Cuba. On that bold assessment of American interventionist sentiment, Taylor concluded the conference believing he had
overpowered the Spanish official as he had the French and British
ambassadors.[38] Loyalty to Democrats and Republicans was dis-
pensible to Taylor; his object was to play a role in freeing Cuba.

In fact, Taylor had succeeded to a degree. Although Spain attempted at least once more to advance the European protest, European diplomats in Madrid refused to join in the agreement during the
remainder of Taylor's assignment. The American minister congratulated himself on this achievement. By disrupting the intrigue he
believed that he had saved the United States from "its greatest humili-
ation in history." Indeed, he made copious notes on the affair, intend-
ing to write an account of his role that would be published posthu-
mously. Although Cleveland did not like Taylor's self-assuming
attitude, the administration did thank him for foiling the scheme.[39]

After traveling to Biarritz, France, where he underwent treatment
for an infection in his blind eye, Taylor returned to work in October
1896[40] His assignment supposedly would last four more months.
During this period he worked enthusiastically for Cuban reforms. To
Spanish officials he presented pertinent portions of Cleveland's last
Annual Message in which the president called for Cuban autonomy.[41]
Wary of American jingoism, the Spanish premier responded by
drafting a bill to increase self-government in Cuba. When Taylor
examined the bill, however, he found it "too vague to inspire confidence in America." Taylor suggested instead that Spain make definite
proposals for virtual autonomy of the island and also recommended
economic reforms beneficial to Cuban trade with the United States.
The premier revised the bill according to this advice. Not until April
1897, however, did the *Cortes* implement these reforms. The Cubans,
anticipating American intervention, kept fighting and awaited a
Spanish-American war.[42]

When William McKinley came to the White House in March 1897,
he was very slow to select Taylor's replacement owing to patronage
squabbles within the Republican party. Unaware of these political
considerations, Taylor interpreted McKinley's inaction on the Madrid post as an indication that his assignment might be extended for
four more years. After all, Senator Lodge knew that Taylor privately
advocated a more aggressive Cuban policy. However, after months of

anticipation, Taylor's hopes were dashed. In June 1897 McKinley advised Taylor that he would be replaced by Stewart L. Woodford of New York.[43] Political patronage in the diplomatic corps, the force that had given Taylor his appointment, had now resulted in his termination.

Before leaving Madrid in September 1897, Taylor devoted a week to advising his replacement on current developments. He told Woodford that a Spanish-American war was inevitable. With characteristic drama, in his final interview with the queen, the former minister expressed similar sentiments. When the queen requested that Taylor "be a friend of Spain" upon returning to the United States, Taylor bowed low and replied: "Madame, I will be so as far as my conscience permits."[44]

Arriving in Washington on October 8, 1897, Taylor immediately presented his final report to the president. He informed McKinley that Spain remained politically incapable of solving the Cuban problem and that violence and destruction would continue on the island until the United States stopped it. Taylor urged intervention, but as the conference broke up, he realized that he had failed to bring McKinley to this viewpoint. The new president was decidedly cool toward him. The following day he tried futilely to see the president again.[45] Ironically, what Taylor had advised McKinley was borne out six months later when the United States went to war over Cuba.

Reflecting on the record of his minister to Spain, former President Cleveland wrote to Richard Olney:

> It was an aggravating thing to have to put up with [Taylor's] general inefficiency. . . . He's another one of our Southern men of "high character" who if appointed "will reflect credit on the Administration." He wrote me that he intends to come to see me. I hope that he will not come.[46]

Taylor did not deserve exactly that type of condemnation. In some respects, as in the case of Spain's attempt to form a European alignment against America's Cuban policy, he performed his duties with great attentiveness, and his continual frustration with Spanish conservatives often made him only appear to be a slow and inefficient worker. What Cleveland perhaps did have a right to resent was Taylor's questionable loyalty to the administration policy. Driven by humanitarian sentiment, a strong strain of New South nationalism, and no doubt an equally strong desire to maintain his limelight job regardless of changed political leadership at home, Taylor all but broke with the administration he had been sent to serve. He had the audacity to espouse American intervention in Cuba while President Cleveland sought a pacific approach to the Cuban problem. This heresy offset whatever positive impression Taylor had previously made on Cleveland. Indeed, even William McKinley, a man highly subject to the expansionist notions of Theodore Roosevelt and Henry Cabot Lodge, had little faith in Taylor's views because of the minister's sensational and unpredictable actions.[47]

Another line of criticism that can be leveled at Taylor's tenure in Madrid stems from his having no experience with Spain and no experience with diplomacy before he assumed the Spanish post. For these reasons Taylor never really understood Spain's position or tactics regarding America's expanding influence. His correspondence and that of his superiors give no clue that Taylor perceived Spanish "procrastination" as it actually was: a design, a rear-guard action, to thwart American diplomatic and economic power in the Caribbean. Instead, he confused Spain's inefficiency with "signs" of Latin inferiority. In discussions with his family, Taylor later would declare that, above all else, he had found Spanish policy makers "inefficient," "indecisive," "weak," and "effeminate." Spaniards had no place in the American realm, the western hemisphere, he concluded.[48] If these views were in part a result of Taylor's environment—intellectuals in late nineteenth-century America were caught up in ethnic perception—Cleveland and the American political process were also to blame for whatever flaws characterized this American mission to Spain. Bowing to pressures to let patronage enter diplomacy, Cleveland had allowed a local lawyer and an individual skilled chiefly in Anglo-Saxon legal history to assume and then maintain a post that increasingly needed an experienced diplomat.

Despite all these drawbacks, Taylor still managed to leave the diplomatic service with a certain sense of success—he had attained national recognition. He felt excited about his reputation as the controversial former minister to Spain. That attention made him want even more recognition as an American of world affairs, and to get it he turned to politics.

IV

Political Aspirant

A MAN LESS AMBITIOUS than Hannis Taylor would have departed from Washington disillusioned with public service and eager to recapture the security of a happy private life. Frustrations resulting from his short diplomatic career, however, only served to whet Taylor's appetite for advancement. Declining an appointment as dean of The University of Alabama Law School, Taylor determined to take his interventionist cause to the people.[1] He believed that the public would applaud his view of American responsibility abroad. Indeed, he believed that Alabamians would elect him United States congressman so that he could play a direct role in the exercise of that responsibility.

Although he had not seen Leonora and the children since June 1896, Taylor remained in Washington during late 1897 in order to write and speak in advocacy of American intervention in Cuba. His first assertion was the most significant. Out of his files Taylor pulled the article Olney had quashed in December 1895. That manuscript represented Taylor's first formal plea for American intervention. Because the Spanish political system lacked the efficiency to solve the problem, declared Taylor, the United States was morally obligated "to itself and to humanity" to intervene and bring reforms to the island. After updating his argument on the ineffectiveness of the *Cortes*, Taylor entitled the manuscript "A Review of the Cuban Question" and initiated plans for publication. The manuscript obviously was controversial, Taylor reasoned; he needed endorsements to publish it at a time when Spanish-American relations became increasingly tense each day. To gain that support he sent copies of the manuscript to three individuals intimately familiar with the Cuban predicament—Senator John Tyler Morgan, who served on the Senate Foreign Relations Committee; Fitzhugh Lee, American consul-general at Havana; and Hilary Herbert, prominent Washington attorney and former secretary of the navy. Taylor chose these readers well. All were Southerners who publicly or privately advocated a greater exercise of American authority abroad. They shared Taylor's nationalistic view of the Cuban problem and encouraged him to

34

publish it as soon as possible.[2] With that support Taylor now felt assured. Indeed, he even sent a copy of the manuscript to McKinley in one last effort to gain the president's ear. McKinley made no reply. Perhaps he feared antagonizing Taylor and prompting the former minister to write an even more sensational piece.[3]

When the article appeared in the *North American Review* early in November 1897, Taylor reaped the attention he had sought.[4] Many national papers praised him for opposing the official Washington policy. Certain New South newspapers went further: they were proud that a man of their region had assumed such a patriotic stance. Cuban refugees in the United States, of course, were encouraged to see Taylor's view in print.[5] Not all reactions to the article served to vindicate Taylor, however. Such antiwar papers as the *Washington Post* and the *New York Times*, as well as several British journals, contended that the former minister should have been more discreet in publishing the information he acquired as an American diplomat. The most emphatic criticism of the article came from Madrid, where government officials viewed Taylor as one who had deliberately misrepresented the condition of Spanish politics in order to force American intervention.[6] McKinley regretted the additional friction which the article caused in Spanish-American relations. Although the president could not publicly censure Taylor, for he had published the article as a private citizen, McKinley did disavow any connection between official United States policy and what he considered to be so blatant a piece of jingoism.[7]

Taylor thrived on the controversy he had caused. In letters published in several New York newspapers, he proclaimed his private right and his moral duty to apprise the public of the real Cuban question. The article had been written, he asserted, in a spirit of "punctilious" patriotism.[8] In mid-November Taylor traveled to Cornell University at Ithaca, New York, to offer further defense of the article. Before a packed audience of 2,000 he reemphasized the sense of morality with which he divulged the ineffectiveness of Spanish decision-makers. Taylor openly criticized President McKinley for rejecting his advice on the Cuban crisis. If the president would allow Congress to vote for intervention, he concluded, "the entire Christian world would rejoice and say 'Amen.'"[9] Taylor intended to deliver a similar address at the Catholic University of America in Washington,

D.C. When the Spanish ambassador, Señor Dupuy de Lôme, heard of that plan, he protested to officials of the university. At the last minute Taylor changed the topic of his speech to avoid the embarrassment of being canceled.[10]

Taylor returned to Mobile on November 28. His family had traveled to Washington to ride home with him. A brass band played the "Star Spangled Banner" and two hundred citizens, most of them Cubans, cheered Taylor as he descended from the coach. On the station platform Mayor J. Curtis Bush formally welcomed Taylor and presented him with a large floral arrangement in the shape of the Cuban star. Taylor then responded to those who he hoped would be his constituency:

> The appeal made to the inmost recesses of my heart by the condition of Cuba caused me to consider whether I could do any good for those . . . bleeding, suffering islanders. My conviction was that without the effort which the heart prompted I should lose all self-respect. . . . Denounced for my private action, I was brought to suffer in this cause. Yet the scars I received are my pride. . . . That my words have aroused a responsive echo in every generous American heart I cannot doubt.

With that Taylor stepped down from the platform and shook the hands of admirers as he made his way to the closed carriage where Leonora and the children waited. After an absence of four and one-half years he returned to his home on Dauphin Street.[11]

In some respects Taylor's return to Mobile proved frustrating. Although he obtained enough legal work to support the family, he experienced difficulty in reviving his law practice because many old clients had found new attorneys during his absence. To compensate for the loss, Hannis joined with his younger brother, George, in attempting to establish a coal export firm. While another brother, Richard, was a successful businessman, Hannis and George lacked the entrepreneurial ability necessary to make the firm prosper. Their efforts in coal exportation lasted little more than a year. That failure was doubly disappointing for Hannis. To pay off his debts he was forced to sell most of a collection of original paintings he had acquired in Madrid.[12]

Still, Taylor had reasons to be optimistic about the future. He remained socially prominent in Mobile, continuing to meet with friends at the Athelstan Club and to participate in Mardi Gras. He felt honored in being elected to the Mobile Commercial Club. Despite the business venture and legal work, he found time to publish the remainder of the manuscript of *The English Constitution;* the second volume appeared in 1898 and received many favorable reviews. He still had sufficient funds to send his family over the bay to vacation in style at Point Clear. Furthermore, the older children—Charles, age nineteen, and Mary Lillie, age fifteen—were emerging as popular young adults whose sophistication complemented their parents'.[13] What most encouraged Hannis about the future, however, was the banquet given in honor of his return at Simon Klosky's Delmonico. On the evening of January 22, 1898, the city leaders sat down to a feast of broiled pompano—the honoree's favorite food—and then proceeded with an hour of toasting. Taylor received laudatory toasts for advocating American intervention in Cuba, and when one guest mentioned Taylor's congressional ambitions, the entire group offered him its full support. Taylor welcomed the backing: "I have had but one passion... to do something for my people... the people of the South."[14]

In fact, Taylor did not wait for the primaries to advance himself as a Congressional candidate favoring a bold foreign policy. In December 1897 President McKinley urged Americans to be patient in dealing with the Cuban problem. When an Associated Press correspondent asked Taylor about his reactions to that address, the Mobilian spared no words. He called on Congress to reject the president's "heartless and selfish" policy towards Cuba. He urged Congress to pass a resolution extending belligerency status to Cuba, for under such conditions the United States might then intervene for the sake of humanity as well as for the protection of American economic interests on the island.[15] Subsequently, Taylor elaborated on these remarks through the columns of a national news magazine, *The Illustrated American.* Under the title "Empire Never Waits," Taylor argued that Americans should control the western hemisphere. In *The English Constitution* Taylor had expounded on the alleged superiority of Teutonic peoples. Since the United States was representative of this group, he now contended that the nation must act according to its "ever-advancing" power and bring Cuba under its economic and political influence. Earlier Taylor had called for intervention on the basis of America's Manifest Destiny. Here he worked to advance his reputation by changing his views according to what he read as the developing popular opinion.[16]

Like many other expansionists, Taylor's philosophy of foreign policy included elements of benevolence. During February 1898, for example, he urged Mobilians to contribute to a Cuban relief fund. If each citizen of the port city would send him one dollar, he announced, he would have sufficient funds to purchase such supplies as food and medicine for war refugees on the island. Taylor's success in this undertaking is not known. By identifying with such a humanitarian cause, he certainly increased his chances for obtaining political office.[17]

Taylor continued to modify his attitudes as America declared war on Spain in April 1898. Fighting lasted less than six months and by February 1899 the United States Senate had ratified the Treaty of Paris, which officially ended the conflict.[18] Throughout that period Taylor employed newspapers, journals, and speaking appearances to keep before the people his ideas on the rapidly developing events. He believed that most Alabamians, like many other Americans, were quickly undergoing a change of thought towards intervention in Cuba. They felt less and less concerned about starvation and killing on the island, he reasoned, and instead demonstrated increasing interest in economic and strategic consequences of the war with Spain. Thus Taylor began to play down his concern for the Cuban people and expressed more and more of an imperialistic attitude towards the conflict.[19]

The Treaty of Paris of 1898 provided for Cuban independence, but subsequent stipulations gave America the right to occupy the island until conditions were stable enough for the establishment of a Cuban civil government.[20] Although Taylor favored passage of the treaty, he criticized provisions for Cuba's total independence. The United States needed to control Cuba, he asserted, to defend the Caribbean and any future isthmian canal. Furthermore, Taylor sympathized with the needs of American investors to regulate the island's enormous sugar output. Regardless of strategic and economic considerations, he believed that Cuba should become American territory because the island was in the Caribbean, within the realm of "legitimate American expansion." Indeed, Taylor felt so strongly about American control over the island that he advocated incorporating it into the Union as a state. Many Southerners opposed Cuban statehood for fear of increasing the "racial mongrelization" of the Anglo-American society. Taylor urged Cuban statehood and still remained true to the racial standards of the New South by calling for the institution of Jim Crow practices on the island.[21]

The Treaty of Paris also provided that Puerto Rico and the Philippines would become American territories. These possessions should be treated differently from Cuba, Taylor contended, and he pointed to the history of the British Empire to demonstrate the need for varying policies for different types of colonial possessions. Since Puerto Rico was located strategically in the Caribbean and within the bounds of "legitimate American expansion," he explained, the United States must maintain strict control over the island. Still, Puerto Rico was too far from North America to function efficiently as a state, so he concluded that a military government served as the only practical means of controlling the island.[22] Taylor urged yet another formula in the Pacific. He did indeed advocate a postwar American presence in the Philippines. He also revered Secretary of State John Hay's Open Door notes of 1899 and 1900, which set America on record as opposing further European partitioning of China. Taylor saw these developments as vital to a check on German expansion, to the extension of American economic interests in China, and, ultimately, to the exportation of American values to China and the uplift of the East. Yet, he argued, the Philippines were situated well beyond America's "legitimate" sphere and should be governed not as a formal American colony but as a protectorate. That type of influence would allow for an American link with the East through naval bases and coaling stations in the islands, but without the problems of financing massive civil and military administration. He pointed to the "revolution" led by Emilio Aguinaldo as clear indication that rigid American control in the Philippines had many problems. In effect, Taylor was expressing a key imperialist litany of the era—strategy, mission, economic self-interest, and efficiency. And by 1902 that mentality would place him in close identification with the supreme personification of the litany, Theodore Roosevelt.[23]

Even before the Spanish-American War broke out in April 1898, Taylor had determined to test the popularity of his imperialist views.

He observed that such Alabama politicians as Senator John Tyler Morgan and Representative Joseph H. Wheeler had found solid support as imperialists. He reasoned that he, too, could be elected to the United States Congress as an advocate of imperialism.[24] Accordingly, on February 5, 1898, Taylor announced his candidacy as a Democrat running for Alabama's First District seat in the United States House of Representatives. That district constituted the counties of Mobile, Washington, Choctaw, Marengo, Clarke, and Monroe. The city of Mobile served as the region's only urban center. North of Mobile stretched the piney woods, with lumber mills and small farms dotting the countryside. Mobile's recent political record was predictable. As a commercial center it had opposed the Populist revolt of the nineties. With one exception, Choctaw County, other portions of the district also followed the rule for much of south Alabama politics. Despite these counties' rural qualities, they had been dominated by strong Democratic organizations and shared Mobile's opposition to Populism during the nineties.[25]

To obtain the Democratic nomination Taylor had to face the incumbent, George Washington "Wash" Taylor, in the September election. The two had little in common. Although Wash Taylor was reared in Mobile, as a young adult he had become an established citizen of Demopolis, a trading center in the northern portion of the district. There his folksy personality and his cunning mind had enabled him to establish a thriving law practice as well as a broad base of support for a political career. In 1896 Wash demonstrated his political talents when he obtained a first term in Congress by vacillating on the currency issue. He appeared conservative enough to carry the district but liberal enough to establish a vague identification with the "free silver" platform of the national Democratic party. The coming election of 1898 he approached with similar strategy. He vacillated on the subject of American intervention in Cuba, talked conservative economics to political leaders in the district, and made occasional "free silver" speeches to court the support of the national party.[26]

In contrast to Wash Taylor, Hannis was a scholarly attorney, a former diplomat, and a representative of Mobile's polite society. His conversation, even more his oratory, was erudite and polished. He had had no experience in politics and was naïve about rural Alabamians. Still, he felt optimistic. By making a strong stand for currency reform he captured the endorsement of Democratic presidential-hopeful William Jennings Bryan. That backing, plus his firm conviction that Alabamians would flock to a noted expansionist, made Hannis certain that he could unseat the incumbent.[27]

The announcement of Hannis Taylor's candidacy aroused little enthusiasm in the northern portion of the First District where Congressman Taylor had a strong organization. Nevertheless, the Mobile *Register* and many citizens of the port city applauded Hannis's bid as did members of the national Democratic hierarchy. William Jennings Bryan, who was then campaigning in the South, came to Mobile to help Taylor kick off the campaign. On March 3 the Hannis Taylor forces held rallies at the Battle House Hotel and the Princes Theatre. Sharing both platforms with Taylor, Bryan spoke for "free silver" and American intervention in Cuba. He implored Mobilians to support Hannis Taylor as the candidate from the First District who best represented these causes.[28] Confident with Bryan's endorsement, Taylor devoted the remainder of March to campaigning in the northern portion of the district. At St. Stephens, Purdue Hill, and Grove Hill he held rallies that drew encouraging responses. During April Taylor limited his campaign appearances to the Mobile area so that he could attend to a backlog of business at the law office. After the outbreak of the Spanish-American War he revisited northern areas of the district, canvassing Choctaw County and returning to Clarke County during June and July.[29]

At Thomasville the two Taylors met for a public debate on July 16. A large group assembled in front of an outdoor platform upon which the two candidates sat. Hannis spoke first. As he left his chair and took two strides to the front of the platform, he appeared impressive. Although he had no sight in his left eye, the lid of which drooped slightly, that was the only imperfection in what his family considered "an otherwise splendid Anglo-Saxon pose." At age forty-seven he had maintained his trim, six-foot figure. His coarse black hair showed slight signs of gray at the temples, and there was a bit of gray in the full moustache he had grown for the campaign. South Alabama seethed with heat in mid-July. Still, Taylor wore a dark suit of clothes, neatly tailored and complete with lapelled vest tidily buttoned from top to bottom. He appeared erudite—and out of place at a Thomasville political rally.[30]

Hannis opened the debate by accusing Wash of not being a silver man at heart but one who simply moved with political winds. Then he launched into what he believed the people wanted to hear, his views on foreign policy. After presenting an elaborate defense of America's "legitimate" rights in the Caribbean, he categorically chastised those who ignored the Caribbean and instead advocated Hawaiian annexation, which represented "illegitimate" expansion into the Pacific. There were few of this type, he admitted, yet he knew of one—Wash Taylor. Concluding, Hannis classified the incumbent as one who had no understanding of American power abroad.

Congressman Taylor next addressed the group. They were a fine bunch, he began, to come to hear him talk on such a hot day. Then he responded to the Mobilian. He believed that south Alabamians had little interest in the former minister's remarks on foreign policy. What concerned Alabamians more, he continued, was honesty in politics; and on the silver issue Hannis had not been honest. The congressman then read aloud a letter from "a New York reporter" who claimed to have heard Hannis refer to "free silver" as "foolishness" while the Mobilian served in Madrid. If Hannis now supported "free silver," concluded the congressman, he had shown himself to be a turncoat and one too unpredictable to represent the people in Washington.[31]

Hannis's rebuttal had no tact. He appeared hurt. How dare Wash accuse him of being inconsistent! His legal career and his scholarship vouched for his intellectual honesty. The congressman was debating unfairly, he continued, by injecting "personalities" into politics. Instead of retorting with specific references to Wash's own inconsistency on silver, Taylor condemned his opponent as one who had failed to keep the campaign "on a high plane of principle and good feeling." Indignantly Hannis shot a final stare at the congressman and stormed off the platform. Wash had no need to offer rebuttal. As the debate ended, the crowd gravitated around jovial, back-slapping Wash, while only a few close friends approached Hannis in an effort to soothe his temper. Wash had shown that he was a good politician. Hannis had appeared erudite and moody.[32]

Despite Hannis's failure at Thomasville, he continued to believe that as an attorney his most effective means of campaigning was public debate. During the next month he confronted Wash on five other occasions. Each ended with results simlar to those of the Thomasville affair.[33]

Taylor probably would have been defeated by political machination even had he been better suited to rural politiking. As the Spanish-American War ended in August 1898, the Democratic Executive Committee of the First District met at Thomasville to organize elections to select delegates for the district nominating convention. Under Wash Taylor's influence, the committee adopted a rule barring all would-be delegates who had bolted to the Populist party in 1896. Because William Jennings Bryan endorsed Hannis as the more sincere silver candidate, the new rule, if implemented, would severely restrict the reform support which Taylor had worked to win. Mobile Democrats forced the State Democratic Executive Committee to annul the rule. Subsequently, Hannis Taylor obtained enough delegates to enter the convention with what he thought was a fair chance of capturing the nomination. Yet the incumbent still had a trick left. When the convention opened at Jackson in September, the Credentials Committee, under Wash Taylor's control, successfully contested the qualifications of nine delegates pledged to Hannis. In their places the Credentials Committee admitted delegates pledged to the incumbent, votes that assured the congressman's renomination.[34] During the week following the convention Hannis Taylor protested the action of the Credentials Committee before the State Democratic Executive Committee meeting in Montgomery. His efforts proved futile. After deliberating throughout the night, the Executive Committee awarded to Wash Taylor enough of the contested votes to guarantee victory. In the end Hannis carried only the delegates of Mobile County and Choctaw County, which was the single county in the district with a strong "free silver" tradition.[35]

Taylor quietly accepted that loss. To further protest the actions of the Credentials Committee, he reasoned, might cause a dangerous rift within the ranks of the Democratic party in south Alabama, thereby enabling a Republican to win the general election. Accordingly, Hannis joined with the Mobile *Register* in endorsing Wash Taylor, who went on to win easily in the November election.[36]

Hannis Taylor would run again. During the next two years he kept his name before the people. Instead of returning to full-time law practice, he managed just enough legal work to support the family and devoted most of his energies to writing and speaking on the merits of American imperialism. Sharing a Boston stage with antiimperialist George F. Hoar, Taylor advanced his notion of "legitimate expansion," carefully stipulating that the theory did not apply to the Philippines. He canvassed his congressional district, too, delivering addresses before such groups as the South Alabama Institute at Thomasville. He showed Mobilians that he remained interested in politics by openly supporting candidates for municipal office. And to stay in the social spotlight Taylor, quite fittingly, served as "Historian of the Empire" during Mardi Gras festivities of 1899.[37]

As Mobilians anticipated, on April 3, 1900, Taylor announced that he would again run against Wash Taylor for a seat in Congress.[38] Hannis reiterated his 1898 platform in calling for "free silver" and endorsing "legitimate expansion." Moreover, he reflected the increasing progressive surge in the South by vaguely advocating stronger regulation of large corporations centered in the Northeast. He was not totally in line with Bryan Democrats, however, as he had been in 1898. Inasmuch as Bryan opposed imperialism in the Caribbean as well as in the Pacific, Taylor's views on foreign policy more closely resembled those of some Eastern Republicans than those of liberal Democrats.[39]

In campaigning Taylor followed the same course he had pursued in 1898. Periodically closing his law office, he ventured off into the upper reaches of the district.[40] As the campaign picked up in June, Taylor wangled an invitation to deliver the commencement address at The University of Alabama in Tuscaloosa. There he appeared before an assemblage of some of the state's most influential people. Speaking on "The Place of the New World in the Family of Nations," he once again enunciated his philosophy of America's right to empire and the need for flexible, efficient colonial administration. He called for the construction of an isthmian canal, predicting that such a waterway would be of enormous benefit to Southern industry and commerce. Taylor hoped that the address would demonstrate his intimate familiarity with foreign relations.[41] Nonetheless, reaction to the speech varied. Several large newspapers in the state praised him as a man of world affairs and great intellectual ability. Gratified to see a Southerner espousing an aggressive foreign policy, the *Boston Herald* noted Taylor's Tuscaloosa appearance and urged Alabamians to elect such an enlightened congressional candidate. The speech did not have the same appeal in most areas of the First District. The rural-oriented Jackson *South Alabamian* cited Taylor's appearance as further evidence of the candidate's elitism, his interest in matters important to urban-commercial interests but matters that had little effect on most of the First District. Thus the Tuscaloosa appearance provided Taylor with some favorable notices but no meaningful advancement of his campaign.[42]

As the summer of 1900 progressed Taylor canvassed more and more of the district's rural communities. His opponent used every opportunity to ridicule Hannis's erudite manner.[43] During August, moreover, Wash effectively employed Protestant fundamentalism to thwart what little chance existed for the Mobilian to win. At the time Hannis did not belong to any church. Because he was married to a Catholic and had numerous Catholic friends, the incumbent managed to convince many citizens living north of the city of Mobile that Taylor was, in fact, a Catholic. In collusion with the congressman's organization, the Jackson *South Alabamian* printed a letter from one J. N. Kidd, a Methodist minister, which condemned the Mobile candidate as a proponent of "popery." Kindled by such incidents, anti-Catholic sentiment became intense. Two weeks before the nominating convention Hannis scheduled a campaign appearance at Citronelle, a normally placid resort town on the northern boundary of Mobile County. His Mobile supporters rallied together a large audience. Before the candidate took the platform, however, several ruffians armed with knives moved through the group promising violence if those assembled did not immediately leave the rally of the "Catholic bigot." The gathering broke up before Taylor could speak.[44]

Although Taylor became enraged over this demonstration of extreme anti-Catholicism, he realized that he must try not to react too strongly. To get the nomination he had to appease some of the people who believed he was a Catholic. Actually, Taylor only alienated them further by announcing that he had never belonged to the Catholic Church or to any church during his adult life. Responding to that declaration, a group of Protestant ministers in the northern portion of the district accused Taylor of being an atheist. Again Taylor overreacted. Arrogantly he retorted that, to the contrary, he was a man of deeply personal religious belief, a man whose thoughts on God were too philosophical to be comprehended by the average man. That assertion of course only brought Taylor more criticism for being out-of-tune with the Protestant fundamentalism of the area. Once more Taylor had been frustrated by his sensitive personality. Again he had suffered because of his political ineptitude.[45]

As the convention drew near, many citizens of Mobile made a frantic effort to swing the rural populace to their candidate. Under the direction of E. L. Russell and Price Williams, campaigners traveled throughout the district to present the facts on Taylor's religion and to portray their man as the type of enlightened leader Alabamians needed in Washington. Those efforts proved futile. On September 18 only the Mobile delegation supported Hannis in the convention, and Wash Taylor was renominated.[46]

Ten days after the convention a *Register* reporter found Hannis Taylor at home on Dauphin Street working diligently on a textbook on international law. The reporter queried Taylor on his reactions to a second defeat. Demonstrating the same moodiness that had contributed to his defeat, Taylor curtly replied, "I am too hard pressed by my present task to look backwards now. My publisher hopes to go to press with the book on January 1, [1901]. . . . I will then return to the bar and devote myself actively to my profession."[47]

Actually, Taylor tried once more to obtain public office in Alabama. Perhaps he would have more success, he reasoned, if he pursued a nonelective office. In the spring of 1901, accordingly, Taylor laid plans for capturing the presidency of the University of Alabama—an appointive post. Mustering new energy, he advanced himself by drawing the support of at least three large newspapers in the state and by appearing before several influential organizations.[48] In June he addressed Confederate veterans from across the state who assembled in Montgomery to honor Jefferson Davis's birthday. Before that group he identified himself with current efforts to disfranchise blacks. Taylor praised the quality of men that Alabamians had sent to the constitutional convention then under way in Montgomery. Certainly these gentlemen would meet their responsibility, he declared, by devising a new constitution that effectively barred the black man from voting or holding office. He explained why black disfranchisement served as the only means to restore honesty and efficiency to Alabama politics. In the end this bid for office proved as fruitless as the others. The Board of Trustees chose a noted professor, William S. Wyman, to be the University's new president. The Board did not want a man like Taylor who had been involved in so much controversy.[49]

Taylor's Alabama political bids provide several insights into Southern politicking at the turn of the century. When he returned from Spain in 1897, Hannis Taylor longed for more national recognition. He believed that he could obtain that reputation as a Southerner by capturing a seat in the United States House of Representatives. He based his campaign for the office on certain elements of the New South creed. He ran as a traditional servant of the Democratic party, the party of the South. As the thrust of his bid, he appealed to nationalistic and racial tenets of the South by advocating American imperialism grounded in a concept of Anglo-American superiority. His notions on foreign policy also served the interests of Southern businessmen then involved in a search for markets. By advocating disfranchisement of blacks, he accentuated the racial viewpoint inherent in his concept of foreign policy. Furthermore, because the New South creed itself contained many contradictions, Taylor could espouse-traditional values while simultaneously calling for change. Thus he advocated two reforms of prime concern to the national Democratic party at the turn of the century—"free silver" and regulation of corporations. In essence, Taylor had reason to be optimistic about his future in politics. On many issues he appealed to a broad sector of white society in the South.

Indeed, Taylor probably would have succeeded in politics had he not lacked certain traits of personality essential to a political victory in rural Alabama. He was not colorful, pragmatic, or shrewd. He was unable to go along with "free silver" and still control the predominantly conservative votes of the First District, as his opponent did. Moreover, Hannis Taylor appeared to be more in tune with the values of upper-class Mobile than with the folkways of rural Alabama. Finally, the religious issue worked against him. He was suspected of being a Catholic in a region dominated by extreme Protestant fundamentalism. Thus the only unwavering political support which Taylor received came from within the city of Mobile, where his upper-class friends, many of whom were Catholic, controlled the Democratic party. These comrades knew Hannis Taylor as an enlightened and warm human being, even if he appeared impractical at times.

In 1901 editor John Rapier asked Alabamians, "Does this state have no need of the services of Hannis Taylor?" After three futile political efforts Taylor believed that he had the answer to that question: his qualities were not those appreciated by most Alabamians. Yet he did not comprehend his lack of appeal. He simply blamed Alabamians for his frustration. He thought that many of the people were intellectually unsophisticated and unappreciative of America's role in world affairs and that they could be base and capable of great personal offense.[50] Although for some thirty years he had found happiness in the South by living in Mobile, he had been disenchanted with the South's rural population ever since his youth. So, in the face of his political failure he decided that his increasing ambitions for the family and for himself would be blocked if he remained in an area dominated by rural values. He continued to practice law in Mobile, but he determined to leave the South at the earliest opportunity.

V

Progressive
Publicist

IN MARCH 1902 Hannis Taylor was offered an appointment as special advisor to American attorneys arguing before the Spanish Treaty Claims Commission in Washington, D.C. That body had been organized to settle claims submitted by private citizens of many countries who lost Cuban investments during the Spanish-American War. Although working for the commission would not provide the prestige Taylor desired, it would serve as an avenue to life in Washington on an adequate income. Taylor accepted the offer.[1]

Moving from Mobile, their home for over thirty years, proved relatively painless for Hannis and Leonora. Editor Rapier wrote that Hannis Taylor was an "ornament to the city" that Mobilians could sorely afford to lose. Rapier urged Taylor to make his move a temporary one.[2] Despite that view, which represented the sentiment of many in Mobile, Taylor at age fifty-one felt compelled to establish a new way of life away from Mobile. In Washington his children could reach adulthood in a more stimulating environment. There, Taylor hoped, his talents would be appreciated. He would become more than just a local ornament. Leonora, too, eagerly anticipated the change. Although moving would separate her from her parents and many old friends, she remembered her earlier experiences in Madrid and looked forward to living in a national capital again.

The Taylors' oldest son Charles would remain in Mobile to work with his uncle Richard at the office of the Mobile and Ohio Railroad.[3] The other four children—Hannah, Mary Lillie, Alfred, and Hannis Joseph—became as excited as their mother when conversation turned to the move to Washington. During the spring of 1902 they enthusiastically helped with the packing of silver, china, and their father's library. By early summer Hannis had sold the home, arranged for other attorneys to take on his clients, and closed the law office.[4]

The Taylors moved in June 1902. Realizing the limits of his modest salary, Hannis purchased a small two-story house on 19th Street in the northwestern section of the District. The family lived there for less than three years. Hannis soon obtained such additional resources

that in 1905 he bought a spacious home on fashionable O Street.[5]
Leonora enjoyed furnishing the new home with antiques and works of
art. Two articles Hannis himself chose and, to Leonora's relief,
proudly reserved for his study: on the wall behind his desk he hung a
huge painting of Lucretia killing herself after being raped by Tar-
quinius, and to the right of his desk Taylor placed a life-size statue of
the crouching Venus.[6]

What gave Taylor the means to purchase another home and to
collect such interesting art was the diversity of enterprises he quickly
assumed upon finding that the Spanish claims did not monopolize his
time. In 1903 Taylor obtained a year's appointment as American
counsel before the Alaskan Boundary Tribunal, a committee established to settle Canadian-American boundary differences on the
Pacific coast.[7] From 1904 to 1906 he served as part-time professor of
constitutional law at nearby George Washington University.[8] When
he stopped teaching he opened a private law practice with offices in
the Maryland Building. After 1910, at which time the Claims Commission adjourned, Taylor devoted full time to his law firm, developing a practice that remained prosperous until shortly before he died in
1922.

In addition, Taylor served as editor of the *American Law Review*
between 1906 and 1907. During his twenty years as a Washington
resident, moreover, he published some seventy articles and pamphlets on history and law as well as five full-length books. His major
writings in this period include *Jurisdiction and Procedure of the Supreme
Court* (1905), *Science of Jurisprudence* (1908), *Constitutional Crisis in Great
Britain* (1910), *Origin and Growth of the American Constitution* (1911),
and *Due Process of Law* (1917). Although these writings provided
Taylor with small but consistent royalties, they were not well received by learned readers. Primarily syntheses of other scholars'
work, his books prompted noted historians and jurists to question
Taylor's intellectual integrity. *Science of Jurisprudence* was particularly
controversial. In it Taylor plagiarized the writings of several English
scholars and for that sin was castigated by both Oliver Wendell
Holmes and Roscoe Pound.[9]

In Washington, Taylor set out to build a new image. He wanted to
be known as an attractive, established citizen of the nation's capital.
Within a year after moving to Washington he had his blind left eye

removed. The operation freed him from the pain that had interrupted his work for years, and the insertion of a glass eye improved his appearance.[10] In building a social life he also worked for a change of identification. Although he maintained a few business and family ties in Alabama, he rarely returned to the deep South. The family vacationed not in Mobile but at fashionable resorts near Capon Springs, West Virginia.[11] Moreover, he made friends with prominent politicians from the East and the West. Senators Albert B. Fall of New Mexico and Thomas H. Carter of Montana became his steadfast friends. He also was quite fond of Senator Henry Ashurst of Arizona and Senator William E. Chandler of New Hampshire, who served as chairman of the Spanish Treaty Claims Commission.[12]

His relationship with Theodore Roosevelt represented Taylor's most gratifying social achievement. In 1902 Taylor met the president through work relating to the Spanish claims. Subsequently, Taylor pursued Roosevelt doggedly and at time with frustration. On one occasion he appealed to Roosevelt's enthusiasm for hunting by purchasing for the president an enormous mounted moose head. Roosevelt would not accept it. "My dear fellow," he wrote Taylor, "I simply haven't room in my house for another trophy. . . . It was awfully good of you to have thought of me." For the great sportsman to have declined such a gift would have represented quite an offense to some, but Taylor would not be discouraged. He continued to court the president's favor, sending violets to Mrs. Roosevelt and congratulating the chief executive on insignificant speeches. Roosevelt appreciated such flattery. He included Taylor in many White House social functions, and even after he left the presidency exchanged views with Taylor on domestic and foreign developments.[13]

By circulating in such an elite society Taylor succeeded in providing his children with social avenues different from those in Mobile. By 1910 both Hannah and Mary Lillie had made debuts. With that formal introduction to the society of Washington, D.C., they were soon courted by young men of the diplomatic corps and other gentlemen of means. Eventually Mary Lillie would marry a Harvard professor and Hannah a Washington businessman.[14] Taylor also provided his younger sons with training for prosperous lives. After sending Hannis Joseph to law school at Georgetown University, Taylor welcomed him into his own law firm in 1915. Alfred attended Dartmouth

College and returned to Washington, D.C., to work with the Bureau of Patents.[15]

In Washington, Hannis also adopted new religious views. He joined the Catholic church, culminating his long-developing estrangement from the Protestant fundamentalism of his youth. In Mobile Father Abram J. Ryan had explained some aspects of Catholic dogma to Taylor. And for many years, of course, Leonora and the children had gently encouraged Hannis to accept their faith. Still, those most responsible for Taylor's ultimate conversion in Washington were faculty members at the Catholic University of America. Taylor found their approach to religion deeply intellectual and very satisfying.[16]

As a teacher and writer Taylor first encountered these clergymen in scholarly circles of the District. He gained an extremely close friend in the University's rector, Thomas J. Shahan, when he managed several legal matters for the school. By 1911 Taylor was taking Sunday supper with the professors and had begun to query them on certain religious and philosophical issues.[17] Soon he pored over doctrinal instructions as if he were readying for a presentation in court. Finally, in 1913 he became a communicant at St. Matthew's Church, where his family had been worshiping since they moved to Washington.[18]

Material, social, and intellectual changes would not satisfy Taylor's drive to be known as a prominent American. He had to play a role in the important public affairs of the era. Thus Hannis Taylor—a Southerner who had come to prominence as a Democrat, indeed, a man who had run for office with the blessings of William Jennings Bryan—determined to identify himself with the political party then in power, the Republicans, and to establish himself as an advocate of an idea then being espoused by that party, progressive reform.

Progressivism was a complex, often contradictory, national reform thrust that gained greatest attention between 1901 and 1917. Although changes in American life were espoused by many sectors of society—farmers, urban laborers, owners of small businesses, large corporations—corporate power often dominated and gave progressivism a basically conservative complexion.[19] Further, under the strong leadership of Theodore Roosevelt corporate progressivism extended the role of the national government in providing gradual solutions for certain economic and social problems of the nation. Roosevelt called for controls over big business, which sometimes produced more stimulation of that business than regulation. He advanced labor reforms sufficient for workers to survive in the new industrial system but not so effective as to allow them actually to change the system. He attempted to make governmental administration more efficient but not necessarily more sensitive to the voting populace.[20] Finally, what enabled Roosevelt to popularize this conservative program was his own dynamic personality. He had spontaneity, vigor, and pungent rhetoric. He preached American superiority and the morality of good citizenship. He excited the people.[21]

Taylor was one of those subject to Roosevelt's powerful appeal. By the beginning of the twentieth century Taylor had developed a sensitivity to the social and economic ills of the country, most of which he attributed to industrialism. Not only did Roosevelt express many of Taylor's concerns about society, but also the president voiced these concerns within the context of American nationalism. Thus Taylor adopted Roosevelt as his leader and became enamored of him personally. As an attorney and constitutional historian Taylor made every effort to identify with the Republicans' corporate progressivism while Roosevelt occupied the White House and for many years thereafter.

Historical writing served as one means by which Taylor asserted his loyalty to Roosevelt's public philosophy. Many progressives, including Albert Beveridge and even Roosevelt himself, wrote of American history in terms of the nation's imminent perfectability.[22] Through numerous articles and one major work, *Origin and Growth of the American Constitution* (1911), Taylor displayed this view as a philosophical basis for progressive reform. He contended that Anglo-American society would maintain its superiority within the context of Charles Darwin's survival thesis. Since Anglo-Americans were biologically superior to other people, he reasoned, then it was predetermined by nature that they would generate the most effective solutions to social and economic problems of the modern world. In addition, Anglo-American law should help provide these solutions. Like Oliver Wendell Holmes and other progressives of the American legal community, Taylor believed that American law as well as governmental administration must undergo continual alteration in order to meet the evolving, constantly changing needs of society.[23]

To demonstrate the origins of American superiority Taylor pointed to the constitutional history of England. Often reiterating what he had written in *The English Constitution*, he contended that the concept of representative government had progressed furthest in the Old World as part of the English parliamentary system. Englishmen had the superior Teutonic blood that enabled them to achieve that plateau. Moreover, as products of the English commonwealth, he explained, Americans also had this "genius for government."[24] Americans had exhibited their governmental talents in the post-Revolutionary era. Taylor believed that experimentation with the Articles of Confederation produced a chaotic government and demonstrated to Americans that their union must be organized under a strong yet flexible government. Hence to Taylor the constitutional convention represented no "mystical experience" in political science. Considering the unique Teutonic talents available to the convention, he explained, it was wholly predictable that the delegates would produce the progressive document they eventually wrote.[25]

Taylor used the history of slavery as an early example of the constitution's progressive characteristics. In the eighteenth and nineteenth centuries, he wrote, most Americans believed in the usefulness of slavery. The constitution reflected that consensus by implicitly providing for the institution.[26] Through the course of the nineteenth century the will of the people nevertheless turned against slavery. More and more people came to view slavery as a cause of social strife and as a force compelling some farmers to depend on an inefficient, one-crop system of agriculture. This attitude even prevailed in the South, he boldly asserted, despite the contrary impression presented by a few proslavery extremists. Thus the federal government functioned under its "organic" constitution, Taylor explained, and abolished slavery through the amendment process. Taylor's reasoning was questionable: he virtually overlooked the fact that the federal government supported slavery through the 1850s and that it worked for abolition only when civil war forced it to do so. Still, in minimizing these factors Taylor further demonstrated his nationalistic view of America's past. In short, he firmly believed in the superiority of the American constitutional system and its ability to advance change. "Nothing has been more remarkable," he wrote in the *North American Review,* "than the ease with which our Federal Constitution has adapted itself to the ever-increasing wants of a rapidly swelling population."[27]

That same nationalistic optimism Taylor applied to problems of industrialism and public policy. He applauded the government's probusiness position of the eighteenth and early nineteenth centuries. The Supreme Court had had the nation's best interest in mind, he suggested, when it supported the doctrine of vested rights in such contract cases as *Vanhorne's Lessee v. Dorrance* (1795) and *Dartmouth College v. Woodward* (1819). He believed that, at the time these noted decisions were handed down, most citizens of the United States still adhered to strict Jeffersonian notions of limited government power. Moreover, such decisions generated confidence in a seminal business life, which needed investments to develop into a strong industrial system.[28] Nonetheless, as industrial growth rapidly increased during the late nineteenth century, he argued, the Court's defense of vested rights no longer had justification. Like Theodore Roosevelt and his spokesman Herbert Croly, Taylor vaguely contended that some corporate monopolies—but not all—had grown too powerful to exert a positive influence on society. That development, coupled with the public's increasing demand for economic reform, prompted Taylor to argue that the Court should use its influence to help change the government's attitude toward economic regulations. As it had moved with public opinion on the issue of slavery, so the government should exercise its flexibility and authority, he concluded, and "help root out the illegitimate elements of America's economic life."[29]

Taylor clearly realized there was need for reform, but when it got down to specific programs his record as an attorney and as a constitutional critic was far less assertive. He lacked depth and consistency. He praised congressional efforts to regulate monopoly through the passage of the Sherman Anti-Trust Act of 1890. He criticized the Supreme Court for its decision in *United States v. E. C. Knight* (1895), which prohibited government regulation over monopoly not actively involved in interstate transportation. Taylor believed that this decision "paralyzed" the Sherman Act and showed the Court to be out of tune with the public need. When the Court gradually assumed an

antimonopoly position, as demonstrated in the Northern Securities
Case (1904) and the first American Tobacco Case (1908), Taylor
lauded the judiciary as the perfect complement to President
Roosevelt's legislative program.[30] Yet, Taylor, like Roosevelt, never
made clear the specific difference between a "legitimate" monopoly
and an "illegitimate" one. If he determined a corporation's legitimacy
by its positive effect on the economy, rather than by its size, then by
what means did he measure that positive effect? In essence, Taylor
left the implication that "legitimacy" was synonymous with
Roosevelt's political needs.

Taylor also appeared uncommitted as an advocate of tax reform.
He blasted the Court for striking down the income tax proposals of
1894. When the nation legalized the income tax by amending the
Constitution in 1913, he praised the entire federal process for its
adoption of that measure. But a desire to reduce the disparity of
wealth in industrial America, a thread that ran throughout much of
the progressives' rhetoric, did not cause Taylor to support an income
tax. He advocated the tax only as a means to preserve the system, not
change it. "So long as we are menaced by the irritating contrast of
great poverty and great wealth," he wrote in 1909, "the socialist and
the anarchist will point eternally to the fact that there is an ultimate
power that can eliminate it all by the destruction of the institutions
that make it possible."[31]

In the same unconvincing way Taylor participated in labor reform.
Vaguely he implored the judiciary to uphold state regulations govern-
ing conditions under which miners might work. He praised Louis
Brandeis's noted brief on better conditions for female workers and
applauded the Court's acceptance of that argument in *Muller v. Oregon*
(1908).[32] Taylor even employed some of the same reasoning as he
argued futilely for the suit of Anaconda Copper Company for the
harmful effects its processing had on farmers working near a smelting
plant.[33] Taylor's reform efforts, however, were not nearly so consistent as Brandeis's struggles. While the nation prepared for World War
I, Taylor successfully defended a West Virginia coal company's fight
against unionization of its employees, and in another case futilely
sought the reversal of a lower court decision that held Tennessee Coal
and Iron Company responsible for hazardous working conditions in
one of its plants.[34]

Taylor's views on railroad regulation reflected more depth if not a total commitment to reform. He criticized the Court for its decision in the Wabash case of 1886, which struck down a state's right to regulate interstate railroads, and expressed equal dissatisfaction over the Court's opinions of the late nineties that destroyed the power of the Interstate Commerce Commission.[35] Furthermore, when Roosevelt attempted to restore ICC powers Taylor rallied to the cause. In 1906 Roosevelt secured passage of the Hepburn Act, which enlarged membership of the ICC, broadened its jurisdiction, and gave it the right to fix reasonable maximum railroad rates. Taylor praised the president's efforts. Still, there were limits to which Taylor would advance railroad regulation. When Senator Joseph W. Bailey futilely attempted to amend the Hepburn Bill with stipulations prohibiting Court interference with the ICC, Taylor dissented along with Senator John Coit Spooner and other Old Guard Republicans. Taylor rushed to the defense of the Court:

> I yield to no man in loyalty to or reverence for that august tribunal, [the Court]. . . . If Congress has the right to cut out the basic principle of the Constitution, [judicial review], then we may begin to speak of the omnipotent Congress as the English speak of the omnipotent parliament.[36]

He urged Congress to reject the Bailey amendment, which it did temporarily. Taylor believed that the Court would gradually move to support railroad regulation.

Although the Supreme Court did not become an equalizing influence in society until after 1937, it did indeed become less antagonistic to railroad regulation after passage of the Hepburn Act.[37] Taylor's faith in "the elasticity of judge-made law" gratified him, particularly because of his developing experience with the Court. He armed himself with an intricate knowledge of the means by which due process clauses in the Constitution had been used to nullify state-level regulatory efforts.[38] Then between 1905 and 1911 he personally tested the Court's changing views on railroad commissions. Taylor won decisions in three of his five railroad cases. As attorney for the defense in *Mobile, Jackson, etc. Railway v. Mississippi* (1908), for instance, Taylor blocked a railroad company from changing construction routes without permission from the Mississippi railroad commission. That body's refusal to grant an alternate route, Taylor argued, did not represent a violation of the company's rights under the due process clause of the Fourteenth Amendment. He also showed that the commission's decision did not stand in conflict with federal jurisdiction over interstate commerce. Finally, he asserted, the commission's action had to be upheld for the public good: a change of routes would virtually destroy the town of Pontotoc.[39]

The satisfaction Taylor derived from his own success before the Supreme Court increased in 1913 when he observed the decision in the Minnesota rate cases. The Court proclaimed that, although the federal government possessed exclusive authority over interstate commerce, a state might act in the realm of intrastate regulation where there was no conflict with federal law. Here, Taylor believed, the judiciary had demonstrated a strong commitment to the enforcement of state railroad regulation, and, waxing eloquent, he compared the justices to "Julianus, Gaius, Papinian, Tribonian, Portolis, Mansfield and Rudolph Sohan."[40]

During the early twentieth century many reformers identified efficiency with progress, and they often did so in most circuitous ways. Taylor was no exception. For a government to work efficiently, he reasoned, it must adapt to society's changing economic needs. He especially criticized legislative inefficiency. In Alabama, Taylor had developed an interest in legislative practices as his preparation of *The English Constitution* led him to study many Old World parliamentary systems.[41] Now, as he lived in daily contact with United States congressmen, Taylor directed his broad knowledge of legislative procedure to the contemporary problems of American government. Taylor showed particular interest in the Keep Commission, the group Roosevelt organized in 1905 to analyze problems of federal administration.[42] In 1908 Taylor directed the commission's attention to the inefficiency of the House of Representatives. An efficient Congress, he asserted, considered as many views as possible on public issues of the greatest importance, and by this standard he accused the House of having been impractical over the past fifty years. Because of the ever-increasing number of bills it had to consider, he explained, the House had attempted to expedite legislative business by granting "titanic" administrative powers to the Speaker. Regardless of who served as Speaker, Taylor continued, his control over the committee system stifled discussion and allowed bills to be advanced with little concern for public priorities. To correct this situation, Taylor recommended implementation of a feature of Swiss parliamentary practice: if Cabinet members could address the House on behalf of certain bills, their presence would direct the legislators' attention to the president's concerns and to issues which the Speaker might have overlooked.[43] Taylor's proposed reform probably would have generated discussion. That it would have increased the efficiency of the democratic process, however, appears at best questionable. The plan simply would have expanded the executive's influence over the legislature. In short, he advocated greater presidential authority to improve representative government, a paradox to which Roosevelt also was subject.[44]

An emphasis on uniform laws represents another aspect of Taylor's efficiency bent. As early as 1881 he warned the Alabama Bar Association about increasing differences of the state codes. Among other consequences, he contended that divergence of standards could create more and more havoc for interstate business.[45] After the turn of the century the states passed an even greater variance of statutes as they advanced economic reforms. Reflecting a concern expressed by many attorneys of the progressive era, Taylor applauded the intent of the states' new laws but viewed their variances as elements of disorder and inefficiency in society. On regulatory legislation, he wrote in 1910, "the states stand to each other . . . like foreign nations."[46]

Through a Harvard law journal, *The Green Bag*, Taylor praised efforts at standardizing the state codes. He was especially proud of changes sponsored by the American Bar Association: thirty-eight states had adopted the Uniform Negotiable Instruments Act; eighteen, the Uniform Warehouse Receipts Act, and six, the Uniform Sales Act. He also noted the endorsement of code reform issued by Seth Low's National Civic Federation. Without the support of President Taft and the Congress, however, Taylor predicted that code standardization would have no broad impact. Fruitlessly he implored Taft to organize an interstate code commission and to serve as its exofficio chairman. Ironically, what Taylor advocated in the area of economic reform—that the Supreme Court should uphold the state's regulatory statutes—helped defeat the movement for unification of

American law. As long as the states found the Court upholding their
varying styles of legislation, they had no immediate incentive to alter
their individual codes.[47]

Taylor's desire for efficiency becomes more apparent in his views
on reform in the South. Even after he had moved to Washington,
Taylor still retained an interest in the region where he had spent most
of his life. Many progressives urged Southerners to improve their
health and educational facilities,[48] but in his later years Taylor displayed more concern with politics and race relations in the South.

The racial views Taylor expressed as a progressive represented an
extension of what he had espoused in Alabama during the late
nineteenth century. Fear of the black had served as a prime feature of
his racial philosophy in this early period. Frightened about the resurgence of black power associated with Reconstruction, Taylor had
advocated segregation to limit nearly every aspect of the black's role in
society.[49] In 1900 he brought this view to bear on the subject of black
voting rights. Delegates assembled in Mongomery to write a state
constitution that would eliminate the black vote. Confederate veterans convened in a nearby hall to give the constitutional convention
their full support on black disfranchisement; and Taylor, invited to
address the veterans, was part of this effort. He applauded the announced purpose of the constitutional convention. He urged delegates to employ literacy and property qualifications to achieve their
goal. These mechanisms, he explained, represented no conflict with
the Fourteenth and Fifteenth Amendments and still provided effective means to eliminate the black vote. If a few whites were also
disfranchised by such stipulations, he concluded, the sacrifice was
worth it. In the end the convention devised a document that did
indeed include these provisions and Taylor felt gratified.[50]

During his Washington years Taylor had little incentive to alter
these views. White superiority was maintained by noted progressive
statesmen, including Theodore Roosevelt.[51] In 1910 Taylor reflected
that bias when he appeared before a Georgetown University commencement and praised the advancement of segregation that had
occurred in the South since he left Alabama. Caught up in the ideals of
economic and governmental reform, Taylor's racial attitude now
stemmed less from fear and more from an appreciation of efficiency.
The effect was the same. Black people he viewed as ignorant and

corruptable; they were a source of disorder in the polity of the state. Yet Southerners had removed much of that inefficiency. Demonstrating their Anglo-American "genius for government and law," they had adopted disfranchisement constitutions throughout the region that effectively eliminated blacks from the voting populace. Hence, while Taylor supported proposals for direct election of senators as an expansion of voting rights for whites, he endorsed severe restriction on voting rights for blacks.[52] In the same vein Taylor praised the efficiency of Southern educational practices. Confident that blacks could make at least some contribution to society—though not through politics—Southern states, he explained, advanced blacks by way of industrial education and thus benefited by the "thrift and industry" of blacks' semi-skilled labor. In essence, here was a progressive's full appreciation of the public philosophy of Booker T. Washington.[53]

On the subject of lynching, Taylor also demonstrated a concern for efficiency. In 1907, as racial violence increased in the South, Taylor analyzed the significance of lynching in an article published by the *North American Review*. Because convicted rapists had unhampered use of appeal proceedings, he argued, these offenders often employed a writ of error to obtain a new hearing, then a new trial and ultimately a new decision overturning their conviction. Hence lynching before the trial, occasionally afterwards, currently served as the white's only effective check on black rapists. While Taylor severely criticized this situation, he showed no concern for the alleged black rapists so often victimized by white mobs. Instead, he deplored the inefficiency of state courts that allowed for free use of appeal in rape cases. "There is something radically wrong with our administration of criminal law," he declared, "[when] the body of the people are driven on particular occasions to take the law into their own hands lest the imposition of a penalty fail altogether."[54]

To remedy the situation Taylor recommended that Southern states as a body adopt a reform recently incorporated into the Virginia state code. Although most states made appeal virtually automatic, in Virginia the argument for appeal had to be presented to the original trial judge. He held power to deny writs of error to those criminals who were, in his opinion, undeserving of appeal, and thus he could easily maintain the original conviction. That reform would eliminate the inefficiency of continual appeal proceedings, Taylor explained, which were expensive as well as time-consuming for a state. Equally important, he concluded, it would help quell the disorder of lynch violence because people would then have faith in their courts' power to deliver effective punishment to black rapists. Although his traditional fear of black assaults on white women was expressed with the clinicism of legal rhetoric, Taylor's views remained well within the Anglo-Saxonism of the era.[55]

Taylor showed equal interest in the South's political progress during the early twentieth century. Because of their experience with Reconstruction, white Southerners had ignored Republican overtures and remained solidly Democratic since the late 1860s. They feared that a split in the Democratic party would prompt a resurgence of the Republican party in their region through which blacks would gain political power.[56] Around 1900 a handful of Southern journalists and businessmen began to call for an end to the solid South.[57] Like them, Taylor argued that maintenance of a one-party system in the South stifled the region, politically and economically. When in 1905 Roosevelt visited in the South, storming across Texas and then making appearances from New Orleans to Richmond, Taylor congratulated the president on his efforts to offer Southerners an alternative in national politics. In a similar way he praised Taft's less colorful but more calculated attempts to crack the solid South.[58]

By 1910 Taylor had assembled a full argument to support the development of a strong Republican party in the South. That year he published in the *North American Review* an article entitled "The Solid South: A National Calamity," a piece that demonstrated the intricate relationship between economics, race, and politics in the South. Taylor admitted that the "Negro question" once justified Southern loyalty to the Democratic party. Since disfranchisement and segregation had removed that "menace," however, he believed that the South now could "emancipate herself from the deadly one-party system." Indeed, Taylor insisted that efficient economic development demanded such a change. The South's industrial growth, he contended, would be determined by its profitable use of foreign markets. In turn, the region's use of those markets depended on its influence in national politics: the more sought after the Southern vote, the more funds for harbor and other export facilities the region would receive from Congress. Therefore, Taylor suggested, Southerners should increase their desirability by responding enthusiastically to Republican over-tures. Such response would encourage President Taft to pursue the Southern vote by sponsoring water transportation bills beneficial to the South, and it would force national Democratic leaders to compete in the same way. At the base of this panacea for Southern backward-ness rested the assumption that the "Negro question" had been solved with the institution of segregation and disfranchisement. Taylor im-plicitly expressed a paradox prevalent in progressive thought: racial discrimination served as an efficient step toward economic and politi-cal progress.[59]

Taylor's views on politics won him considerable recognition; he was classified with Walter Hines Page and Edgar Gardner Murphy as an intellectual Southerner who offered acute insight into his region's recent past. Regardless, what he and a few others espoused had little impact on voting patterns in the South. Fearful of the Negro and bound by tradition, Southerners remained solidly Democratic until the second half of the twentieth century.[60]

Because he sought a position in the mainstream of American life, Hannis Taylor embraced what he viewed as the symbol of American nationalism—Theodore Roosevelt and his publicly espoused reform philosophy. Like his hero, Taylor viewed American history not only as evidence of the nation's superiority in the world but as reason to believe that planned, efficient change could bring added improve-ments to the American way of life. In advocating change Taylor also reflected many of the contradictions that characterized Roosevelt's elitist, corporate breed of progressivism. Taylor criticized corporate power. Except in the case of railroads, however, he remained vague in discussing specifically what types of industrial power should be re-formed, and he called for revisions of state codes, which would aid the operation of powerful interstate businesses. Further, he wrote in advocacy of labor reforms but managed suits filed to prohibit such reforms. He called for an income tax, not out of concern for poverty but out of fear that the poverty stricken would revolt against capitalism and turn to socialism. He advocated increased democracy in public administration through the adoption of efficiency reforms that would expand executive authority. He urged the South to take on a more efficient system of economics and politics; yet he endorsed the noted racial "reforms," segregation and disfranchisement, which helped tie the South to its traditional backwardness. Although Taylor called for the development of a better America, he refused to make the sacrifice of laissez faire values upon which that progress depended. His personal views exemplify the contradictions that barred progressivism from realizing many of its goals and demonstrates the essentially conservative character of national progressivism.[61]

Taylor was not troubled over these contradictions; like many other progressives he exhibited no awareness of them. Instead, he lived a happy life in Washington, D.C. He brought four of his five children into adulthood as citizens of the capital, sending them on their way in that cosmopolitan society. There, too, Taylor advanced himself intellectually, socially and professionally. He embraced what he considered an intellectual and in other ways deeply satisfying dogma—Catholicism—which marked his ultimate rejection of the Southern Protestant fundamentalism that he had so long abhorred. He developed fast friendships with noted political figures from the East and the West, most of whom were Republicans. He served as an active participant in a highly publicized reform movement. In some ways he shed his reputation as a Southerner and took on the identity of a prominent citizen of the nation's capital.

In 1908 Theodore Roosevelt congratulated Taylor on his role as an American:

> I have always taken pride in your having played the role you have in public life, because there are not too many Americans who can both do their work in politics and diplomacy and at the same time do totally different work of real value in the field of literature and history.[62]

Meeting Theodore Roosevelt's standards for good citizenship provided the ultimate sense of accomplishment for Taylor. He had pride in his role as a progressive on the domestic scene and felt encouraged to make a further contribution in the field of foreign affairs.

VI

Progressive Looking Outward

IN HIS ANNUAL MESSAGE of 1902 President Theodore Roosevelt declared that "the increasing complexity of international relations renders it incumbent on all civilized and orderly powers to insist on the proper policing of the world."[1] With the same idealistic rhetoric that he employed to encourage domestic reform, Roosevelt called on the United States to bring order and "civilization" to world affairs. Yet, Roosevelt's approach to foreign policy frequently appeared inconsistent and at times contradictory. In European and Asian affairs he worked for a balance of power as the key to world progress. In the western hemisphere he worked for United States control as a means to "civilized" diplomacy. At times he identified American conquest, military occupation, and economic control with the advancement of mankind, and for that chauvinistic attitude he incurred the criticism of such noted antiimperialists as William Jennings Bryan and Tom Watson.[2] Still, the crusading, nationalistic speeches that Roosevelt used to justify his foreign policy received general approval across the country, especially among progressives in the urban East. Indeed, his preachings on the United States' predestined role as the reformer of world affairs contributed greatly to Roosevelt's reputation as one of the most popular spokesmen of American nationalism.[3]

With few exceptions Hannis Taylor supported the nationalism of Roosevelt's foreign policy. Between 1901 and 1908 Taylor employed his talents as a writer and as an attorney to publicize Roosevelt's efforts abroad. He lent similar support to President Taft. In 1912 Taylor temporarily parted with the Republicans and supported Woodrow Wilson for president, but within two years he had returned to the Republican fold as a critic of Wilson's Mexican and European policies. After differing with Roosevelt on the draft, Taylor joined Roosevelt in opposing the League of Nations, labeling it an international organization that would destroy American self-determination. After Roosevelt died in 1919, Taylor continued to support Republican foreign policy during the early twenties.

Although Taylor's first position in Washington had no more than a vague relationship with Roosevelt's foreign policy, it did enable him eventually to obtain an important appointment under Roosevelt. In 1902 Taylor had moved to the capital to assume an assignment as special counsel before the Spanish Treaty Claims Commission.[4] The Treaty of Paris of 1899 obligated the United States to settle personal and property claims of Americans against Spain, which originated during the late Cuban revolution. When President Roosevelt followed McKinley's plans by sponsoring the Spanish Treaty Claims Commission to hear these cases, the Justice Department engaged Taylor to refute those claims appearing invalid. The work proved boring and undramatic. Between 1902 and 1910 Taylor, with five other government attorneys, confronted petitions for awards totaling over 62 million dollars and nullified all but $1,300,000 of that amount.[5] In 1906 the government received severe criticism for its frugality. Through the *North American Review* Taylor responded to this dissatisfaction, arguing that the commission's decisions demonstrated the efficiency of the Republican administration.[6]

Former Senator William E. Chandler of New Hampshire, chairman of the Spanish Treaty Claims Commission, developed a strong liking for Taylor. Indeed, when Hannis's brother, Richard, general manager of the Mobile & Ohio Railroad, brought his private railroad car to Washington to give Hannis a luxurious fifty-sixth birthday party, the Taylor brothers invited only one guest to the all-night fête. The esteemed guest was William E. Chandler.[7] More important, Chandler quickly gained respect for Taylor's legal and speaking abilities. An influential Republican, Chandler urged Roosevelt to give Taylor a substantial role in the administration. Roosevelt knew of Taylor's expansionist sentiment from his activities at the outbreak of the Spanish-American War. Like Chandler, the president was impressed with Taylor's oratorical abilities, having observed several early sessions of the claims proceedings.[8]

Consequently, in 1903 Roosevelt appointed Taylor as one of the three attorneys to present the American case before the Alaskan Boundary Tribunal. That body had been established by agreement of the United States and England to solve the increasingly tense conflict over control of inlets that served as entrances to the Alaskan gold fields. Americans maintained that the inlets were theirs according to the Alaskan purchase of 1867; Canadians—still British subjects—contended that the inlets were property of the Dominion by virtue of an Anglo-Russian treaty of 1825.[9] A pro-American decision was inevitable. England did not want to offend the United States at a time when she was incurring greater and greater competition with Germany in Africa. Moreover, of the six members of the tribunal, three were ardent Rooseveltian expansionists—Senator Henry Cabot Lodge, former Senator George Turner, and Secretary of War Elihu Root—and a fourth, Lord Richard E. W. Alverstone, sided with the Americans. Even so, Roosevelt intended to use oral arguments of the proceedings to assert American strength in the affairs of the western hemisphere. He needed a strong personality to present an aggressive image of the United States. Taylor would serve that purpose.[10]

Taylor eagerly accepted the appointment. With the other American attorneys, Jacob M. Dickinson and Charles Anderson, Taylor appeared before the tribunal convened in London during September and October of 1903. He effectively argued against application of the Anglo-Russian treaty and presented an intricate analysis of the history of the two-mile line that constituted the Canadian-American boundary along the disputed section of the coast.[11] More important, he argued with the same type of blustery rhetoric which Roosevelt himself often used in assertion of American power abroad. When British attorneys supported their argument with inaccurate maps of the coastline, Taylor lambasted their efforts as an attempt to employ "an artificial creation which bears no more relation to a natural boundary than a Hyperion to a Satyr."[12] Towards the end of oral arguments Taylor debated the usage of the term coastline. While British attorneys maintained that a political coastline could on certain occasions run behind a geographical one, Taylor cited numerous authorities to prove the contrary. He concluded the rebuttal with a flurry of dramatics:

> I respectfully call upon the representatives of Great Britain... to search the international jurisprudence of the world and see if they can prove from the treatise of *any* publicist in *any* nation that *anybody* has put into *any* book *anything* in the way of an authority for [Britain's] contention [regarding the term *coastline*.][13]

Finally, Taylor summed up his two days of presentation with a typically bold assertion. He recalled asking the English scholar Edward A. Freeman for an opinion on the writings of historian James Anthony Froude. "If you ever read anything he writes," Freeman responded, "read it with care . . . for then you will know one thing for certain—by no possibility did it happen this way." That, concluded Taylor, was the assessment which the Tribunal must reach after hearing the British argument.[14]

Shortly thereafter the Tribunal adjourned to deliberate. Having to return to Washington and the Spanish claims work as soon as a decision was rendered, Taylor used that ten-day adjournment period to celebrate the victory he so eagerly anticipated. The royal family received him as an eminent American attorney and scholar of English history. He toured country estates outside London. He even reserved enough theater boxes for the entire American delegation to the Tribunal to enjoy an evening of drama as his guests.[15] On October 20, 1903, America was awarded the unbroken strip of coast which it had contended was its rightful entrance to the gold fields. Reveling in his role in the American victory, Taylor returned to Washington where he received a personal expression of appreciation from the president.[16]

If in London Taylor reflected Roosevelt's personal aggressiveness, Taylor demonstrated through his writings on American foreign policy a doctrinaire adherence to Roosevelt's notion that the United States must control the western hemisphere. Like his president, Taylor believed in the righteousness of American continental expansionism during the eighteenth and nineteenth centuries.[17] That Anglo-Americans enjoyed a biological superiority over other people, Taylor contended, had been demonstrated by their westward surge to the Pacific coast despite Indians and environmental hazards. Yet, he explained in the *North American Review*, the world had not taken note of American superiority in the western hemisphere until Thomas Jefferson, "the wisest and strongest expansionist," cast aside "constitutional quibbles" and purchased Louisiana. Twenty years later, in 1823, promulgation of the Monroe Doctrine served as formal notification of United States hegemony in the West. William H. Seward had shown the strength of that policy in his Mexican and Alaskan policies; and in 1895, Taylor asserted, Grover Cleveland and Richard Olney had given the doctrine full expression when they intervened in the Venezuelan boundary dispute.[18] Taylor's views on the Spanish-American War were well known. As one who had participated in the diplomacy of the era and who lauded the new empire, it was predictable that Taylor, writing in 1905, could look back on the Spanish war with a sense of supreme nationalism. That conflict, he explained, served as the most dramatic signal of America's power abroad and its control of the western hemisphere. He summarized the significance of the war:

> Let us make no mistake; let us indulge in no self-deception. This aggressive and rapidly advancing nationality is neither cowardly nor incompetent. It does not propose to shrink from the discharge of any of the high duties that destiny has put upon us.[19]

The same chauvinism appeared in Taylor's writings on Roosevelt's own activities in the hemisphere. Latin American nations, reasoned Roosevelt, were "too uncivilized" to govern themselves. Thus American intervention in those countries, he believed, was justified not only in the cause of efficient government but also in an effort to maintain stability in the western hemisphere, which would discourage European intrusion. Demonstrating this conviction, Roosevelt arbitrated the Venezuelan debts dispute of 1902 and intervened in Cuba and Santo Domingo in 1906.[20] Taylor praised the president's actions and sought active participation in further arbitration negotiations.[21] With the Second Pan American Conference scheduled to convene in Mexico in 1906, Taylor applied for an appointment as a United States delegate to the meeting. There he intended to support Argentina's Luis M. Drago, who advanced arbitration as the most effective solution to hemispheric disputes. Taylor did not receive the appointment. Nevertheless, when the conference endorsed Drago's doctrine, Taylor praised the meeting through the columns of the *American Law Review*. Arbitration in the western hemisphere, in Taylor's view, meant United States mediation.[22]

Particularly satisfying to Taylor was the notion that Roosevelt "took" the Panama Canal. Roosevelt's efforts to dig an isthmian canal seemed stymied in 1903. Suddenly a revolution in Panama, executed with Roosevelt's cognizance and American naval protection, made that Colombian province an independent republic. Immediately, Panama encouraged construction of the American canal. With little regard for offense such negotiations would represent to Colombia, Roosevelt forthrightly dealt with the Panamanians, and canal construction got under way.[23] Crediting the president with having instigated the revolt, Taylor dubbed this act as "Roosevelt's masterful stroke at Panama." He equated Roosevelt's roughshod tactics with Jefferson's bold purchase of Louisiana, both acquisitions reflecting a "prescience almost supernormal." The canal would increase American trade in the Orient, he asserted, and facilitate the movement of the American navy between the Philippines and the Caribbean, a strategic boon essential to proper maintenance of American hegemony in the western hemisphere.[24]

Taylor also endorsed Roosevelt's approach to the "insular question" in the Caribbean. Roosevelt maintained that Puerto Rico, which had been an American possession since the Spanish war, should not be given statehood or any rights associated with that status.[25] Before he moved to Washington, Taylor had assumed the same attitude. He continued to defend the notion as the question of constitutional rights for Puerto Rico came before the Supreme Court during the early 1900s. He applauded Court decisions upholding the legality of import charges on Puerto Rican goods shipped to the United States. Such policies benefited North American businessmen; and after all, he concluded, Puerto Rico's predestined function was to serve in that capacity.[26]

In his attitudes towards America's role in the Pacific, Taylor went even further in echoing Roosevelt. American control of the Philippines must be maintained, Roosevelt asserted, not just for economic reasons but as a strategic check on German expansion. Granting constitutional rights to Filipinos would undermine that control, Roosevelt believed, and Taylor agreed.[27] Especially offensive to Taylor was the antiimperialist view espoused by Supreme Court Justice David Brewer. When Brewer dissented against the majority opinion in *Dorr v. United States* (1904), which upheld strict protectorate status for Filipinos, Taylor questioned Brewer's patriotism. Such critics as Justice Brewer, Taylor wrote in the *North American Review*, refused to acknowledge that "our maintenance of territorial governments in distant dependencies are predestined and settled elements in our national life."[28] Roosevelt appreciated the backing and reciprocated. In 1911, when Taylor applied to President Taft for a position on the Philippine Commission charged with supervising Philippine affairs, Roosevelt gave him his hearty endorsement. He even enlisted the aid of other prominent Republicans on Taylor's behalf. By this time, however, the breach between Roosevelt and Taft had developed too far for that support to be effective. As one closely associated with Roosevelt, Taylor was denied the appointment.[29]

Roosevelt's approach to Oriental and European affairs did not appear as blatantly imperialistic as did his policies for the western hemisphere. He worked for a balance of power in the Old World, which would bring stability to relations marred by conflict and disorder and would deter Japanese or German aggression in the American realm.[30] To achieve this goal Roosevelt assumed a leading role in the international arbitration movement. He worked hard to advance the Hague Conferences, meetings at which major powers agreed to organize machinery necessary for the maintenance of international peace. The first of these conferences, held in 1899, established the Permanent Court of International Arbitration; six years later the second meeting attempted, with little success, to give meaningful authority to the newly created court.[31]

Taylor, like Roosevelt, viewed the accomplishments of the first Hague Conference with great optimism. "As nations become more perfectly organized," Taylor proclaimed, "they will perceive that stability and economy may be promoted by a transition from the reign of arms to the reign of law."[32] To assure that the conference of 1899 marked a turning point in diplomacy, Taylor, writing in 1902, urged the second meeting to adopt the concept of "limited compulsory arbitration." Here he reflected Roosevelt's desire that signatory nations should be bound to the decisions of the court as long as their "national honor," their very existence, was not at stake. Furthermore, Taylor called on the upcoming Hague meeting to adopt resolutions for arms limitations, as did the president. Finally, Taylor supported Roosevelt's concerted effort to give Hague representation to Latin American countries and to the Papacy. That particular cause succeeded at the 1907 meeting, whereas, to Taylor's disappointment, movements for arms limitation and compulsory arbitration failed.[33]

Roosevelt publicized Hague ideals and worked actively at applying these standards. In 1905 he served as third-party arbitrator in the Russo-Japanese conflict, and the following year he brought a settlement to German, French, and English claims over Morocco in north Africa. During the same period, furthermore, Roosevelt negotiated arbitration treaties between the United States and major powers of the world, as did Taft in 1911.[34]

Taylor applauded Roosevelt's commitment to making peace. Resolution of the Morocco crisis was particularly impressive, he felt, because it included the notion of "spheres of influence." He believed that the establishment of such colonial boundaries would allow colonization to continue uninterrupted by international conflict.[35] With similar idealism he lauded the arbitration treaties. If America submitted its "noncritical" disputes to a third-party arbitrator, then other countries would be encouraged to use America as a mediator. This was the country's predestined role in world affairs, Taylor proclaimed in *The Green Bag:*

> I cannot doubt that it is the present paramount duty of the people of the United States to give to this movement in favor of limited compulsory arbitration . . . the entire weight of its moral influence. That something we call destiny was not acting blindly when it planted this great Republic here in isolation, midway between Europe and Asia, so it might become the most independent and therefore the most potentially arbitrating power in the world.[36]

As the presidential election of 1912 approached, Hannis Taylor temporarily parted with the Republican party and moved back into Democratic ranks. Republican politics were in the throes of disruption: conservatives renominated Taft for the presidency; liberals, splitting off to form the Progressive party, advanced Roosevelt for a third term. Although Taylor was endeared to Roosevelt, the increasing divisiveness and backbiting of Republican politics frustrated Taylor's constant search for popular causes. In reaction, Taylor became caught up in the campaign of another progressive candidate, Democratic nominee Woodrow Wilson.[37] Besides his broad popularity, Wilson attracted Taylor because he was a Southerner. Taylor had not maintained many close ties with the South since leaving Alabama a decade earlier. Still, he kept an acute interest in Southern political power on the national scene as he had revealed in 1909 by pleading for an end to the solidly Democratic South as the most efficient means for the region to regain an influential role in national political life. Now he aimed at the same goal, the return of the South, but pragmatically ignored the means he earlier had prescribed. Instead, he viewed Wilson's election as the surest path to a resurgence of Southern political influence as well as a new opportunity for the advancement of his own career.[38]

Joining Walter Hines Page and other Southern expatriates, accordingly, Taylor worked with loyal Democrats to place a Southerner and a reformer in the White House.[39] Taylor contributed a moderate sum to the Wilson campaign fund. The Democratic heirarchy, nonetheless, wanted something else from Taylor. A Wilson endorsement from a prominent member of the Roosevelt camp, and a Southerner at that, would provide a meaningful boost to the Democratic effort. Hence powerful Democrats living in Washington, D.C., invited Taylor to serve as keynote speaker at a local rally organized to raise funds for the general election. Taylor accepted the offer and hoped to get something out of it. During October 1912 he went before an assemblage of Washington's finest. He praised Woodrow Wilson as a man of great moralistic leadership and as a man whose view of government closely resembled that of Theodore Roosevelt. The difference between Wilson and Roosevelt, he explained, was that Roosevelt did not have the unified party support necessary to advance another successful administration; but Wilson enjoyed great popularity among Democrats as well as some support among splintering Republicans. Because of his political advantages and progressive philosophy, Taylor concluded, Wilson should be elected the next president of the United States. Many shared Taylor's view. Wilson won the presidency in 1912.[40]

For a short while after the election Taylor continued to show interest in the Democratic party. To obtain an appointment in the new administration he attempted to reestablish himself as a Southerner, since the South had given such solid support to Wilson. In January 1913, as the inauguration approached, Taylor sent Wilson a lengthy letter concerning the appointment of cabinet members. Two Southerners who qualified for and deserved the office of attorney general, Taylor asserted, were Senator Hoke Smith of Georgia and Representative Robert L. Henry of Texas, both proven progressive reformers. Taylor offered this suggestion out of pure interest in the success of the administration, he wrote, for he personally was not a candidate for any political position.[41]

Several months later Taylor applied for the position of special counsel to the State Department.[42] He had little chance of getting it. Wilson feared Taylor's close association with Roosevelt. Moreover, the new president, like Cleveland and McKinley some fifteen years earlier, looked upon Taylor as a sensationalist, one too excitable, too emotional to serve in the crucial position of special advisor to the secretary of state. Finally, at least one noted scholar, Edward S. Corwin of Princeton University, informed Wilson that Taylor was not a man of intellectual integrity. Much of Taylor's recent writing in constitutional history, Corwin claimed, showed signs of plagiarism. Wilson had no intention of appointing a person of questionable ability and vacillating loyalty to the Democratic party. Instead, he gave the special counsel position to John Bassett Moore, an eminent scholar of international law. Taylor considered the selection of Moore to be a personal affront.[43]

The breach between Taylor and Wilson widened during the spring of 1914. Believing that the United States should compensate Colombia for the means by which Roosevelt had acquired the Panama Canal, Wilson sponsored the Thomson-Urrutia Treaty providing for payment of 25 million dollars and an official apology from the United States.[44] Taylor had lauded Roosevelt's actions in Panama. Nevertheless, during 1913 he came to view Colombia reparations as a popular cause. For that reason, as well as the chance of obtaining a large fee, Taylor agreed to serve as counsel for Colombia in the treaty proceedings.[45] When it was rumored that Taylor would receive one million dollars for these services, the president condemned Taylor as one who took advantage of America's desire to rectify a grave error. Wilson implored Taylor to perform his duties gratis, to be a patriot dedicated to the improvement of United States-Colombian relations. Before Senate hearings in 1914 Taylor flatly denied that he had been promised a sum even one-fourth as large as reports indicated. Furthermore, he announced, his fee would not be definitely set until the Thomson-Urrutia Treaty had been ratified by the Senate. Whatever "just" fee he received at that time was his private business with Colombia and with no other government. In 1922, after discovery of oil in Colombia, Senate Republicans finally allowed ratification of the treaty and Taylor received $25,000. Yet, Wilson offended Taylor in 1914 by suggesting that he provide his services without charge, and the attorney bore a grudge.[46]

Taylor had committed heresy for a member of the Roosevelt camp. He had supported Wilson in 1912 and sought a role in the new administration; then he had worked on behalf of a treaty that implicitly renounced Roosevelt's acquisition of the Panama Canal. Never again would Roosevelt consider Taylor his friend.[47] Despite that, within two years after Wilson's election, Taylor began to seek reidentification with Roosevelt. The former president personally disliked Wilson, as did Taylor. Then, too, Roosevelt led the opposition to much of Wilson's foreign policy, reflecting an extreme nationalistic outlook that had long been Taylor's. In essence, while Roosevelt had come to view Taylor as an unpredictable sort, Taylor never stopped admiring the vigorous, patriotic image maintained by Theodore Roosevelt.

Even before Taylor split with Wilson in 1914, he had begun to oppose certain administration policies, notably the president's position on the Panama Canal tolls question. The Canal Act of 1912 exempted American coastal shipping from paying tolls, and England criticized it as a violation of the Hay-Pauncefote Treaty of 1901, which guaranteed equal rates for all ships using the canal. Although Wilson had supported exemption during the campaign of 1912, he changed his position upon assuming office and worked for repeal of the Canal Act.[48] Like Roosevelt, Taylor viewed Wilson's new position as a relinquishment of American control in the Caribbean and launched a protest against nullification of the exemption act.[49]

Taylor first had shown hostility to the British position while Congress worked at passing the Canal Act. When Britain protested the proposed legislation, Taylor, writing in *National Waterways* magazine, labeled that criticism as "inane."[50] Now, as Wilson pressured Congress to repeal the act, Taylor appeared before the American Society of International Law, convened in Washington, D.C., and offered more substantive support of the exemption. He explained that the United States had predestined rights to control the Caribbean. Yet, even without these rights America had no obligation to maintain equal rates for use of the canal because the Hay-Pauncefote Treaty was not binding. According to the international doctrine of *rebus sic stantibus*, he expalined, treaties ceased to be binding when the conditions under which they were signed ceased to exist. When America signed the 1901 treaty she had no intention of purchasing the canal zone; now that she had made that purchase, the conditions of America's role in the Caribbean had so changed that the Hay-Pauncefote Treaty was automatically abrogated. With this weak argument Taylor urged that Wilson cease efforts to force revocation of the tolls exemption act. And if England persisted in the matter, he concluded, the controversy should be resolved through "diplomatic negotiations," as Roosevelt had managed such matters. In late 1914 Wilson succeeded in having Congress repeal the controversial act.[51]

Taylor could not criticize Wilson's intervention in Santo Domingo and Haiti, for in many ways those actions represented an extension of Roosevelt's own Caribbean policy. Yet, he did find flaws in Wilson's Mexican policy and wasted no words in villifying it. When Wilson assumed the presidency in 1913, Victoriano Huerta ruled Mexico. Huerta encouraged American oil investment in Mexico, but Wilson nevertheless refused recognition of Huerta's government because of its authoritarian characteristics. Indeed, during 1915 Wilson intervened at Tampico to protest Mexico's harsh treatment of American sailors, and the same year Wilson authorized American occupation of Vera Cruz in order to block a German arms shipment bound for Huerta's forces. A hemispheric conference at Niagara Falls forced Huerta's resignation in 1916, but Wilson's Mexican problems continued with Pancho Villa's raids on American citizens living near the Rio Grande. On Wilson's orders, American troops pursued Villa for more than a year. They were called home in February 1917 when the president began to give full attention to the European War.[52]

Writing in 1916, as American forces chased Pancho Villa, Taylor asserted that "no American can look upon the Mexican [policy] without a sense of pain."[53] He reflected Roosevelt's view: Wilson had failed to assert American honor and superiority in Mexico.[54] After having spoken idealistically about the wrong of American intervention in Mexican affairs, Taylor explained, Wilson had intervened. Moreover, once Wilson had established an interventionist policy, he had been unable to carry out that policy with any degree of effectiveness. Huerta had been defeated ultimately through the combined presence of the hemispheric nations, not through United States influence. When American citizens appealed to their government for protection from Pancho Villa, Wilson sent an insufficient number of troops into Mexico. Wilson's "spasmodic fits and starts" in Mexico, Taylor believed, showed America to have a "nervous, fidgety, and irresolute" chief executive. How different, as Taylor saw the two, were Roosevelt and Wilson![55]

With similar antagonism Taylor villified Wilson's European policy. Especially repugnant to Taylor was the president's defense of the rights of neutrals in time of war. In late 1914, as the European war expanded, England blockaded German ports, subjecting the neutral American ships trading with Germany to a severe "search and seizure" policy. In reaction, Germany established a war zone around the British Isles in early 1915, which also discriminated against supposedly neutral American ships trading in the area. Although Wilson protested against the actions of both nations, his statements were not strong enough to force the belligerents to make permanent changes of policy.[56]

Like Roosevelt, Taylor hated the idea of America being bullied by other countries.[57] He considered Wilson weak. In a paper presented to the Alabama Bar Association in 1915, Taylor advised fellow attorneys that "the fundamental and unchangeable law of nations [that of neutrality] is now being set aside and trampled upon just as if it did not exist at all." This situation was "an offense to American manhood," he asserted. To counteract it, Taylor suggested, on other occasions, that the United States should cease supplying war material to Britain.[58]

Protecting national pride was not the only reason Taylor criticized Wilson's irresoluteness toward Europe. Although Taylor had moved away from the South, he remained interested in that region's economic advancement and became distraught about the effect of the war on cotton exportation. Before Alabama attorneys he recounted England's promise not to discriminate against Southern cotton. Despite that pledge, cotton had been placed on the contraband list in an "appalling, indefensible, and flagrant" violation of Anglo-American trust. The South suffered, he concluded, and Woodrow Wilson— who had received such solid support from the South—made no effort to correct the situation.[59]

England offset resentment about the cotton crisis by negotiating large purchases of cotton and by manipulating international cotton prices to the benefit of Southerners. That development, coupled with Germany's increased use of submarine warfare, brought the nation into an increasingly pro-Allied attitude during late 1915 and early 1916. Responding to that sentiment, Wilson sponsored limited measures in preparation for American intervention in the war. Still, during the presidential election of 1916, Republicans led by Roosevelt lashed out at Wilson as one who opposed complete preparedness and thus as one whose support of the Allied cause was questionable. Wilson responded by maintaining that if possible he wanted a world peace that did not result from further war.[60]

Taylor echoed Roosevelt's criticism of Wilson. During the fall of 1916 Taylor appeared before the National Republican Committee, convened in New York City, and endorsed Charles Evans Hughes for president.[61] His position resulted more from his dislike of Wilson than his admiration of Hughes. Taylor chastised the president for holding back preparaedness through extreme use of executive authority. He portrayed Wilson as one determined to rule America as a monarchy, as one who had no respect for the will of the people or for the sentiment of Congress. His disregard for the populace, Taylor suggested, had been made abundantly clear after Germany's sinking of the *Lusitania*:

> We have been outraged and trampled upon. . . . The mangled bodies of American men, women and children . . . have floated away unavenged. In response we have had notes, notes, notes, like Amos Cattle's poem, with "lines forty thousand, cantos twenty-five" . . . We have only responded with paper bullets bearing the inscription, "Too proud to fight!"[62]

When the United States finally went to war, however, Taylor did not remain the extreme patriot. Increased German submarine warfare, the Zimmermann note and other factors finally led Wilson to go before Congress on April 2, 1917, and ask for a declaration of war against Germany. Congress not only gave Wilson that declaration but also subsequently passed a conscription program to support the war effort. Roosevelt reveled in this militarism. Taylor dissented from one aspect of it.[63]

Unlike some Southerners who opposed American intervention as a conspiracy perpetrated by powerful business interests,[64] Taylor supported the general war effort but criticized a particular feature of the conscription plan. On constitutional grounds he opposed sending National Militiamen to fight overseas. Following passage of the Selective Service Act in May 1917 Taylor severely criticized the law's application to these soldiers. As his writings appeared in the antiwar *LaFollette's Magazine* and in the *Congressional Record*, Taylor's arguments displayed a lucid appraisal of the draft as a constitutional issue and also showed the vehemence with which he viewed Wilson's enforcement of the act's militia clause.[65] Even so, Taylor presented his most comprehensive critique of the militia issue before the United States Supreme Court when he served as counsel for the appealee in *Cox v. Wood* (1918).[66] That case represents Taylor's most significant effort as an attorney.

In December 1917 Robert Cox, a member of the National Militia, received orders under the recently passed Selective Service Act to report to Camp Funston, Kansas, to prepare for overseas duty. Upon arriving at camp, Cox protested to the Commandant, General Leonard Wood, that as a member of the National Militia he had no obligation to perform military duty outside the boundaries of the nation. Wood rebuffed Cox and the young soldier filed suit. By the spring of 1918 the case had worked its way to the Supreme Court, at which stage Taylor was retained to present Cox's argument.[67] In the meantime, during December 1917, the Court had heard challenges to the overall constitutionality of the new draft law. On the grounds that Article II of the Constitution gave the president the power to raise and command an army, the Court upheld the legality of the Selective Service Act.[68]

Cox v. Wood came before the Court on April 17 and 18, 1918. First, Taylor delved into the constitutional history of England to demonstrate that national militia traditionally served only on the home front. When England finally determined to send national militia to France in 1916, Taylor asserted, she realized that such an action represented a breach with precedent and, unlike the United States government, she felt compelled to justify it through constitutional amendment. Next, Taylor traced the English tradition in American constitutional development. He showed clearly that the constitutional convention of 1787 had intended to limit the role of the National Militia to domestic duty. He quoted from Article I of the Constitution: "The Congress shall have the power to provide for calling forth the [national] militia to execute the laws of the Union, suppress insurrection and repel invasions." By contrast, he continued, other branches of the military—the Regular Army and the State Militia—were specifically designated for duty abroad. Finally, he described uses and opinions of the militia clause in the Constitution, all of which further illustrated that the National Militia was not to go overseas. In fact, he cited four speeches delivered by Wilson during 1916 in which the president himself gave this assessment of the militia's role. Now Wilson was contradicting himself, Taylor proclaimed. Without the necessary constitutional amendment, Wilson was attempting to send the National Militia to Europe on the basis of his executive authority.[69]

To those who maintained that the president's actions were justified through the recently rendered Selective Service Cases, Taylor correctly responded that the Court had in no way considered the question of National Militia in its earlier deliberations on the draft. Indeed, if the Court used these cases to deny Mr. Cox his rights, Taylor argued, it would be guilty of "a desperate and transparent assault on the Constitution." It would be granting "autocratic military power" to a "wicked" president who viewed law with "total contempt."[70]

John W. Davis, attorney for the government, briefly retorted that the Selective Service cases had, in fact, settled all questions related to the draft and that Taylor's argument was irrelevant. Furthermore, he considered Taylor's presentation to be "impertinent" and "scandalous"; it represented "a gross attack on the government."[71] The Supreme Court agreed. Several members of the Court, especially Oliver Wendell Holmes, had never liked Taylor because of his blustery style and questionable integrity as a constitutional scholar. Moreover, the court was infected with the same extreme patriotism that gripped so much of the nation during the war. In the midst of Taylor's argument Holmes had leaned over to Justice Willis Van Devanter and whispered, "Taylor is a pig-headed adherent of an inadequate idea."[72] Thus the unanimous decision rendered against Taylor represented more of a rebuke than an expression of legal logic. Totally ignoring Taylor's argument, Chief Justice Edward D. White denied Cox's exemption from overseas duty on the basis of presidential powers included in the Selective Service Act. He then censured

Taylor for criticizing the United States government with "unwarranted" and "intemperate" terms.[73]

Taylor was distraught over the Court's illogical decision and deeply hurt over the challenge to his patriotism.[74] As in 1912, he had separated himself from the Roosevelt standard and had been rebuffed. That would never happen again. During the last four years of his life Taylor worked to reassert his image as an unflagging Rooseveltian nationalist. As the controversy over the League of Nations developed, he found an ideal opportunity to pursue such an identification.

Even before America entered the war, Taylor, like Roosevelt, criticized Wilson's notion of a League of Nations.[75] On January 22, 1917, President Wilson went before the Senate to explain his plan. He called for the establishment of an international court which, unlike the Hague, would have extreme powers in settling diplomatic disputes before they erupted into violence. The following day, as many Democrats heralded their leader's foresight, Taylor joined Republicans in pointing to Wilson's naïveté.[76] In a special interview with the *New York Times* Taylor explained how the president's plan would give second-rate powers equal force in world affairs with such leaders as the United States and England. That conflicted with Taylor's belief that the more "civilized" nations should determine the course of world events. Furthermore, Taylor asserted, Wilson's League would allow European nations the right to settle disputes in the western hemisphere, a direct violation of the Monroe Doctrine, and would bring America into the entanglement of European alliances. Demonstrating his usual flair for words, Taylor concluded that the League represented "a paroxysm of insanity" and offered further evidence of the president's "dementia."[77]

With war concluded in 1918 and Wilson announcing plans to attend the Versailles conference so as to advance the League personally, Taylor struck similar notes. At the request of Republican Senator Lawrence Y. Sherman of Illinois, Taylor presented to the Senate a full critique of the president's intention to go abroad. Article II section 10 of the Constitution, he explained, provided that the president's duties devolved to the vice-president whenever the chief executive could not perform all the functions of his office. Accordingly, as soon as Wilson embarked for Versailles, contended Taylor, Vice-

President Thomas R. Marshall should be sworn in as president. Despite similar protests from noted Republicans, Wilson maintained his office and worked diligently to mold the League into the treaty.[78]

Theodore Roosevelt died on January 6, 1919. Although he had stated privately that he would support the League with certain modifications maintaining American control in the Caribbean, in public he had issued blanket criticism of the plan.[79] Taylor took these public expressions at face value. With his hero's death, Taylor determined to carry on the Rooseveltian tradition by advancing the uncompromising criticism of Woodrow Wilson and the League. Wilson brought the treaty home for Senate ratification in the spring of 1919. Taylor used the columns of the New York *Herald* to reassert the League's conflict with Roosevelt's Caribbean scheme. By giving Europe decision making power in Latin American affairs, he argued, the League invited a conspiracy between Europe and Latin America to destroy America's control over the western hemisphere.[80] Moreover, he aligned himself with Senator Miles V. Poindexter, William E. Borah, and other "irreconcilables" as the Senate began debate on the treaty, supplying these Republicans with anti-League arguments to be employed in the hearings. In one such piece Taylor accused Wilson of being bribed by England and France to force the League on the American people. Finally, on November 19, 1919, the Senate defeated the treaty. Taylor felt exuberant. His view of the League—and what he thought Roosevelt's view to be—had been upheld by a majority of the members of the United States Senate.[81]

Between 1920 and 1922 Taylor suffered increasingly from the afflictions of Bright's disease, anemia, and high blood pressure. Despite that, he continued to work as a publicist of the Republican party. As the election of 1920 approached, he made numerous compaign appearances in the Washington area on behalf of Warren G. Harding.[82] Senator Henry S. New and other Republican friends promised Taylor that he would be rewarded with an appointment in the new administration, probably a position on the staff of the attorney general. When Harding won the election in November 1920, Taylor received no such prize. The new attorney general, Harry M. Daugherty, looked upon Taylor as a man with significant limitations: he was sixty-nine years old and ill. Wanting not just a loyal staff but one that could effectively advance the politics of "normalcy," Daugherty denied Taylor the position.[83]

Taylor refused to admit that his career had come to an end, despite Daugherty's pronouncement. He was physically ill, granted, but his mind remained sharp. Still eager for an appointment under Harding, Taylor campaigned for the Republicans in the congressional elections of 1922.[84] He gave particularly strong support to Harding's sponsorship of the Washington Conference for international disarmament held during 1921–1922. In a series of articles printed in *The National Republican*, a shortlived party organ, Taylor contended that by bringing Asia and Europe to disarmament agreements, America had exercised her duty as a world leader to help bring order to international affairs. Certainly, he proclaimed, this stand represented no retreat from responsibility as some Democrats contended. Indeed, Harding's "epoch-making" foreign policy served as "a resumption of America's normal diplomatic relations with Europe and Asia" as that policy had been advanced under Theodore Roosevelt's progressive leadership. Taylor's articles were read aloud in the Senate. He was applauded. And still he received no appointment.[85]

That was Taylor's last attempt to obtain a further role in Republican politics. His health prohibited another effort. Indeed, during the congressional campaigns in 1922 Taylor's blood pressure rose so high that he was forced to stay in bed for several days.[86] His law practice dwindled, and his income dropped to almost nothing. Then, suddenly, his financial condition was rescued. In April of that year the Senate had bowed to pressures from American oil interests in Latin America and agreed to ratify the Thomson-Urrutia Treaty, granting Colombia 25 million dollars but withholding the apology for America's crude acquisition of the canal route. Eight months later, in October 1922, Taylor finally received his controversial $25,000 fee. Moreover, he could now accept the much-needed funds with a clear conscience. Henry Cabot Lodge, Roosevelt's heir to Republican party leadership, had argued for ratification of the treaty, claiming— accurately or not—that Roosevelt himself would have voted for the treaty, considering America's great benefit from the canal since 1914.[87]

For more than twenty years Hannis Taylor reflected the progressive doctrine of foreign relations espoused by Theodore Roosevelt. As an attorney, journalist, and scholar, he lauded Roosevelt's administrative policies; he supported Taft's programs, which he understood to be an extension of Roosevelt's; and, later, he joined Roosevelt in opposing Wilson's diplomacy. In the main Taylor was happy in that role. Although he functioned on the periphery of the Roosevelt circle, he befriended Roosevelt for a while and became close to other prominent Republicans of the era. Identified with these policies and these personalities, he believed he lived in the mainstream of the American way of life. Indeed, when he felt compelled to venture away from the Roosevelt standard—first during the election of 1912 and later during the draft crisis of 1917-18—he did so only for a short while, always rushing back to the Roosevelt cult with new enthusiasm.

By pursuing such an identification Taylor entangled himself in contradiction just as he had done in advocacy of domestic progressivism. Although America's westward movement all but destroyed an Indian culture, he praised America's continental expansion for the "civilization" which it bestowed upon others. Despite the fact that Roosevelt's tactics of intervention and economic control wrought dissension and authoritarianism, Taylor extolled Roosevelt's control of the western hemisphere for the progressive stability it brought to the area. Although Roosevelt advanced arbitration and international organization only so long as American prestige and economic power abroad were maintained—establishing influences that ultimately would help frustrate the cause of international peace—Taylor applauded Roosevelt's efforts to resolve European and Asian conflicts as genuine reform in international affairs. Hence Taylor's views reflected the myriad of contradictory forces that contributed to origins of modern American foreign policy. Roosevelt showed an amazing awareness of some of these contradictions; he looked upon them as evils necessary to man's gradual advancement.[88] Taylor, by contrast, showed no awareness of them. As he approached the end of his life he looked back on his last twenty years as the decades in which he had helped espouse the perfect solutions to conflict within the international community. He was the idealistic progressive.

In late November 1922, Taylor, at age seventy-one, entered Washington Sanitorium, his affliction with Bright's disease having severely worsened. His kidneys functioned poorly, his blood pressure was critical, and he was too weak to sit up.[89] On December 21, when doctors informed Leonora that Hannis would live only a short while longer, she called the children to the hospital. The family began staying with Hannis in shifts. He became weaker and weaker, entering a coma on the day after Christmas. On December 27 he died peacefully with Leonora and the two girls beside him.[90]

Two days later, on Friday morning, a requiem mass was held for Taylor at St. Matthew's Catholic Church. Bishop Thomas J. Shahan, Taylor's close friend, officiated with assistance from Monsignor Edward L. Buckey. Following the service, the body was taken to Rock Creek Cemetery in the District where it was placed in a vault until other arrangements could be made for interment at nearby Fort Lincoln Cemetery. Those who came to the funeral included such prominent Republicans as Senator Henry S. New of Colorado and Supreme Court Justice George L. Sutherland of Ohio. Perhaps another Republican, Theodore Roosevelt, also would have attended had he not died some three years earlier.[91]

Epilogue

DURING THE LATE nineteenth century and on into the mid twentieth century, many Americans embraced the myth that their way of life, their society, approached perfection: they were conditioned to believe that few were hungry; that government was sensitive to the masses; that people of different races lived in harmony even while separated; and that Americans were not only overcoming the problems of industrialization but also were using technology to form a society that had no equal in the history of the "human race." For only a small portion of the Americans was this image a reality. Yet, compared to those in other regions, fewer Southerners could approach the promised life of opulence and security and moral gratification. The South's experience with slavery, its defeat in Civil War and Reconstruction, its reluctance to industrialize, and its tightly closed political system—all these factors combined to generate more enduring poverty, racial strife, and political elitism than in other areas of the country.

How significant this Southern experience actually is remains a matter of considerable contention. C. Vann Woodward has suggested that, because post-Civil War Southerners shared a history so at odds with the optimistic American creed, they had the potential to assume an iconoclastic attitude towards the myths that so often frustrated efforts to reform American life. In advancing a public policy some Southerners, for instance, might have realized that Americans as a whole would obtain a decent standard of living only when capitalism was subjected to effective regulation. They might have attacked such cultural myths as Anglo-Saxon racial superiority and supplanted them with more egalitarian social doctrines. They might even have advanced a foreign policy aimed earnestly at peace and coexistence rather than toward the extension of the American system abroad.[1] That did not happen. Throughout the late nineteenth century and on into the twentieth century few indeed were the Southerners who exhibited a realistic attitude toward their environment. And why the Southern iconoclasm failed to develop is a problem into which Hannis Taylor's experience bears insight.

Taylor matured in an environment that might have provided him with a critical view of American life. Granted, some of the misfortunes of his youth resulted from personal experiences—the loss of an eye, sudden family deaths, a father who could not manage business affairs. Yet, certain of Taylor's childhood experiences came directly from his living in the South during Civil War and Reconstruction. He heard the booming artillery as it bombarded the area around New Bern. He witnessed the blood and mangled limbs of soldiers being brought from the front. He observed the actual surrender of a major portion of the Confederate army. He had to move constantly throughout the war as his family fled from Union troops. While his father's failure as a provider helped defeat Taylor's college ambitions and left the family in continual financial straits, factors external to the Taylors' personal situation—the war-torn state of the South and poor employment opportunities in the region—also contributed to their misfortunes. Thus the violence, disruption, poverty, and frustration of Taylor's youth could have affected his attitude towards the South and, in turn, could have influenced the way he viewed the nation. As an adult he might have been cautious about accepting the creed that American life approached perfection. Taylor developed that discerning viewpoint only to a limited degree.

Although he always remembered his Civil War experience and maintained an abiding interest in the economic, racial, and political developments of the South, Taylor's strong ambition and his subjection to national ideals compelled him to cast aside his potential skepticism and to embrace the myths of American nationalism as might one from New England or the Midwest. As a proponent of the New South movement he espoused the contradictory views often associated with the South but which, as events in the 1950s and 1960s demonstrated, were more accurately a reflection of national myths accepted by many throughout America. He believed that racial harmony and advancing economic standards could exist alongside racial discrimination and that socially responsible government could be generated from politics controlled by vested interests. As a diplomat he came to accept the notion that America's imperial control over other people represented no conflict with democracy. After moving to Washington, Taylor continued to cling to these tenets of Americanism. As a progressive he had faith that the nation would cure its social and economic ills without sacrificing its laissez faire values and corporate-controlled public policy. He identified efficiency with progress. Finally, he assumed that America's predestined role as a world power was to bring efficiency and stability to international relations and to create an order that would be receptive to the social values and business practices of industrial America. As a progressive he would have America uplift the world.

Taylor's career prompts a speculation. If Taylor was a representative New Southerner, and he seems to have been one, then it appears that the skepticism which a Southerner might reflect because of his regional experience is offset by other factors not directly related to regional background. Obviously one's personality could help nullify regional experience. If a Southerner aspired to great reputation, as Taylor did, he could have felt the need to plunge into the mainstream of national life and in the process to disregard certain realities of his life in the South. More important, during the late nineteenth and early twentieth centuries American nationalism became so potent that it could have counteracted whatever uniquely regional attitude Southerners might have otherwise developed. With Civil War and Reconstruction concluded, industry undergoing rampant expansion, and the United States exercising a new and powerful role in world affairs, many Americans assumed a blind faith in the superiority of American life. Such nationalism had enormous appeal to Hannis Taylor, a patriotic New Southerner. It caused him to ignore the significance of his early years and to seek an identification with such contradictory figures as Theodore Roosevelt. Perhaps the nationalism of that era affected other Southerners in a similar way.[2]

Whatever the broader significance of Taylor's views, his life in personal terms represents a tragic, if relatively common, ordeal of human beings who are highly ambitious. Hannis Taylor devoted his adult years to pursuing recognition as an eminent American. Popular causes, he believed, were his vehicle to fame. Employing enormous energy, forceful rhetoric, and a facile pen—he published eight books and one hundred articles—Taylor sought identification with what he considered to be the popular trends in American intellectual life, domestic policy, and foreign affairs. As a constitutional historian he espoused the nationalism and Anglo-Saxonism so prevalent in his day. As a proponent of the New South movement he echoed views

expressed by Henry W. Grady and Walter Hines Page. As a
nineteenth-century expansionist he reflected the chauvinistic concepts of Henry Cabot Lodge and Theodore Roosevelt. During the
progressive era he publicized Roosevelt's conservative notions on such
topics as corporate regulation and international affairs. Despite his
identification with these causes, however, Taylor never obtained the
reputation to which he aspired. Through his endeavors as a diplomat,
attorney, and writer he became known in some prominent circles, but
he failed to attain the eminence enjoyed by those he emulated. His
frustration in that regard did not result from a lack of determination,
to be sure, or from limited ability. Rather, his flaw lay with the
zealous, impulsive, self-assuming qualities of his personality. He
rallied to so many causes so quickly that he could not obtain the
respect commanded by men of more depth and stability.

Hannis Taylor had insight into human strivings for achievement,
even into his own. "I am more and more impressed," he wrote in 1899,
"with the vanity of human ambition. For men who think they can
build a temple of fame to perpetuate their memory are foolish."[3] Still,
it was, sadly, his tragedy that he could not satisfy his own deep yearn-
ing for fame. Until the year of his death, Taylor's Christmas Eve
celebration included gathering the family around him and instructing
one of the older children to read aloud from the scrapbook of newspaper clippings that told the story of his multifaceted career.[4]

Notes

Chapter I

1. Hannis Taylor, "Vivid Pictures of Old Times in New Bern," *North Carolina Review*, August 7, 1910, 11.
2. Hannis Taylor, *Origin and Growth of the American Constitution* (Boston: Houghton Mifflin Co., 1911), 338–41.
3. Mary L. Taylor Hunt, "Memoirs of a Diplomat's Daughter," 1 (MS in possession of author); Thomas M. Owen, *History of Alabama and Dictionary of Alabama Biography* (4 vols., Chicago: S. J. Clarke Publishing Co., 1921), IV, 1649; memo in Issac Taylor Papers (Southern Historical Collection, University of North Carolina, Chapel Hill, North Carolina); *Manuscript Returns on the United States Seventh Census, 1850* (National Archives Microfilm Publications), Schedule I, Free Inhabitants in the County of Craven, State of North Carolina, 592.
4. "Hannis Taylor," *National Cyclopaedia of American Biography* (13 vols., New York: James T. White and Co., 1900), VIII, 118 (hereafter cited as *NCAB*); Richard V. Taylor, "A Voice from Alabama: An Autobiography Which Includes a Record of a Journey from a Cooper's Bench to a Seat on the Interstate Commerce Commission," ch. 1, p. 3 (MS in possession of the heirs of Helen Taylor Abbot, Mobile, Alabama). Richard's younger brother, William Taylor, would become a well-known North Carolina surgeon and inventor.
5. Mary L. Taylor Hunt to Tennant S. McWilliams, April 1, 1969 (personal letter in possession of author and in the collection hereafter cited as Hunt-McWilliams Correspondence); Richard V. Taylor, "Voice from Alabama," ch. 1, p. 1; *Manuscript Returns on the United States Seventh Census, 1850*, Schedule I, 592.
6. Hunt, "Memoirs," 1; Richard V. Taylor, "Voice from Alabama," ch. 1, pp. 4–5.
7. Unidentified newspaper clipping in Isaac Taylor Papers; Richard V. Taylor, "Voice from Alabama," ch. 1, pp.4–5.
8. Deed Register of Craven County, North Carolina (Office of County Clerk, New Bern, North Carolina), Book 62, 367–74; newspaper clippings in Taylor Family Bible (in possession of heirs of Helen Taylor Abbot, Mobile, Alabama).

9. Mary Bryan Hollister, untitled MS on the Taylor family in Isaac Taylor Papers; Elizabeth Moore to Tennant S. McWilliams, January 11, 1972 (personal letter in possession of the author and in the collection hereafter cited as Moore-McWilliams Correspondence).

10. E. Wilder Spaulding, "Hannis Taylor," *Dictionary of American Biography* (22 vols., New York: Charles Scribner's Sons, 1936), XVII, 326–27 (hereafter cited as *DAB*); Richard V. Taylor, "Voice from Alabama," ch. 1, p. 14.

11. The other Taylor children included Richard Stevenson (b. 1853, d. 1853), Mary Hooper (b. 1855, d. 1876), Cornelia Wilson (b. 1857, d. 1858), Richard Vipon (b. 1859, d. 1939), James Stevenson (b. 1861, d. 1923), Hannah Willard (b. 1864, d. 1869), George Stevenson (b. 1866, d. 19?), William Caird (b. 1868, d. 1906). "Family Record," Taylor Family Bible; Richard V. Taylor, "Voice from Alabama," ch. 1, pp. 1, 14, ch. 2, p. 1, ch. 3, p. 3.

12. Deed Register of Craven County, North Carolina, Book 62, 367–74.

13. Taylor, "Vivid Pictures of Old Times in New Bern," 11; William H. Oliver, comp., "Centennial Commemoration of New Bern Academy" (New Bern, 1906), 2, 4, copy in R. A. Nunn Papers (in possession of Elizabeth Moore, New Bern, North Carolina); Frances Beverly, "Hannis Taylor," 1, MS in Records of Historic Mobile Preservation Society (Oakleigh House, Mobile, Alabama).

14. Mary L. Taylor Hunt to Milo B. Howard, Jr., June 18, 1966 in Hunt-McWilliams Correspondence; Hunt, "Memoirs," 1.

15. Mobile *Register*, August 12, 1900; Hannis Taylor to Cornelia Phillips Spencer, October 2, 1880 in Cornelia Phillips Spencer Papers (Southern Historical Collection, University of North Carolina, Chapel Hill, North Carolina); Mary L. Taylor Hunt to Tennant S. McWilliams, April 1, 1969 in Hunt-McWilliams Correspondence; Richard V. Taylor, "Voice from Alabama," ch. 1, pp. 9–10; newspaper clipping in Taylor Family Bible; Susan Stevenson Taylor to Helen Stevenson————, May 3, 1868, copy in Hunt-McWilliams Correspondence.

16. Taylor, "Vivid Pictures of Old Times in New Bern," 11.

17. John G. Barrett, *The Civil War in North Carolina* (Chapel Hill: University of North Carolina Press, 1963), 96–113; Kemp P. Battle, *History of the University of North Carolina* (2 vols., Raleigh: Edwards and Broughton Co., 1907, 1912) II, 474.

18. Richard V. Taylor, "Voice from Alabama," ch. 1, p. 8; Taylor, "Vivid Pictures of Old Times in New Bern," 11; Barrett, *Civil War in North Carolina*, 367–97.

19. Richard V. Taylor, "Voice from Alabama," ch. 1, pp. 5–8; North Carolina Department of Archives and History to Tennant S. McWilliams, August 22, 1972. It is not known how Richard Taylor avoided military service.

20. See Hope Summersell Chamberlain, *Old Days in Chapel Hill: Being the Life and Times of Cornelia Phillips Spencer* (Chapel Hill: University of North Carolina Press, 1926).

21. Cornelia Phillips Spencer Diary, January 17, 1867, and Cornelia Phillips Spencer to Dr. [Alexander] Wilson, March 7, 1866 in Spencer Papers; Chamberlain, *Old Days in Chapel Hill*, 126.

22. Hannis Taylor to Cornelia Phillips Spencer, October 2, 1880 in Spencer Papers.

23. Hannis Taylor to Jacob M. Dickinson and David T. Watson, June 10, 1903, and Hannis Taylor to Jacob M. Dickinson, July 6, 1903 in Jacob M. Dickinson Papers (Tennessee State Archives, Nashville, Tennessee); Hunt, "Memoirs," 6.

24. Mary L. Taylor Hunt to Milo B. Howard, Jr., June 18, 1966 in Hunt-McWilliams Correspondence; Hunt, "Memoirs," 1.

25. Beverly, "Hannis Taylor," 1; Spaulding, "Hannis Taylor," *DAB*, 327; Cornelia Spencer to Alexander Wilson, March 7, 1866 in Spencer Papers; Battle, *History of the University of North Carolina*, I, 460, 476; Susan Stevenson Taylor to Helen Stevenson————, May 3, 1868, copy in Hunt-McWilliams Correspondence.

26. Faculty Minutes [for 1867] of the University of North Carolina, 321 (Southern Historical Collection, University of North Carolina, Chapel Hill, North Carolina); *Sketches of the History of the University of North Carolina, 1789–1889* (Chapel Hill: The University, 1889), 217; Battle, *History of the University of North Carolina*, I, 775, II, 41, 75.

27. Alfred R. Taylor, "Reminiscences [of Hannis Taylor]," 14 (MS in Southern Historical Collection, University of North Carolina, Chapel Hill, North Carolina); University [of North Carolina] Student Records, 1852–1868 (Southern Historical Collection, University of North Carolina, Chapel Hill, North Carolina); Battle, *History of the University of North Carolina*, I, 772–73.

28. Philanthropic Society Library Records, 1866–1871 (Southern Historical Collection, University of North Carolina, Chapel Hill, North Carolina).

29. Register of the Members of the Philanthropic Society, 53; Philanthropic Society: Signatures of Members, 1867, 1875–1886, 1; Philanthropic Society Treasurer's Book, 1859–1869, 469; Philanthropic Society Minutes, 144 (Southern Historical Collection, University of North Carolina, Chapel Hill, North Carolina).

30. Cornelia Phillips Spencer, "Chapel Hill, North Carolina Commencement, 1892," *North Carolina Presbyterian*, June 8, 1892; *Atlanta Constitution*, March 11, 1900; Mobile *Register*, April 7, 1893; Susan Stevenson Taylor to Helen Stevenson———, May 3, 1868; copy in Hunt-McWilliams Correspondence.

31. Hollister MS in Isaac Taylor Papers; Richard V. Taylor, "Voice from Alabama," ch. 14, p. 6; *Branson's North Carolina Business Directory* (Raleigh: Branson and Jones, 1868), 34.

32. Oliver, "Centennial Commemoration of New Bern Academy," 4.

33. Ibid.; Maud M. Washington, comp., "John N. Washington," MS in Washington Family Papers (in possession of Elizabeth Moore, New Bern, North Carolina); "Hannis Taylor," unidentified sketch in Records of Historic Mobile Preservation Society (Oakleigh, Mobile, Alabama); Mobile *Register*, April 7, 1893.

34. Washington, "John N. Washington," 2.

35. Hannis Taylor to Mrs. F. C. Roberts, [n.d.] in F. C. Roberts Papers (in possession of Elizabeth Moore, New Bern, North Carolina); Mary L. Taylor Hunt to Tennant S. McWilliams, January 21, 1972 in Hunt-McWilliams Correspondence; Richard V. Taylor, "Voice from Alabama," ch. 1, pp. 9, 12–13.

36. "Hannis Taylor," *NCAB*, 118; "Hannis Taylor," in Records of Historic Mobile Preservation Society; Richard V. Taylor, "Voice from Alabama," ch. 1, p. 9; unidentified newspaper clipping in Taylor Family Bible.

37. Mary L. Taylor Hunt to Tennant S. McWilliams, April 1, 1969 in Hunt-McWilliams Correspondence; Spencer, "Chapel Hill, North Carolina Commencement, 1892"; Richard V. Taylor, "Voice from Alabama," ch. 1, pp. 1–13, ch. 3, p. 4.

Chapter II

1. *United States Ninth Census, Statistics for the Population of the United States* (Washington: Government Printing Office, 1872), 81; Walter L. Fleming, *Civil War and Reconstruction in Alabama* (New York: Columbia University Press, 1905), 733–92; Horace Mann Bond, "Social and Economic Forces During Reconstruction in Alabama," *Journal of Negro History*, XXIII (July 1938), 336–43; James G. Randall and David Donald, *Civil War and Reconstruction* (2nd ed., Boston: D. C. Heath & Co., 1961), 562, 599–600, 619.

2. Quoted in Allen Johnston Going, *Bourbon Democracy in Alabama* (University, Ala.: University of Alabama Press, 1951), 5–6.

3. Peter Joseph Hamilton, *Mobile of the Five Flags* (Mobile: Powers Printing Co., 1913), 356; Fleming, *Civil War and Reconstruction*, 671–73.

4. Going, *Bourbon Democracy in Alabama*, 6–8; Hamilton, *Mobile of the Five Flags*, 347; Hannis Taylor, "A Political History of the State," *Memorial Record of Alabama*, (2 vols., Madison, Wis.: Brant and Fuller, 1893), I, 92.

5. Mobile *Register*, November 11, 1890; Owen, *History of Alabama*, III, 33, 171; *Mobile City Directory, 1870*, 179, 205; *Mobile City Directory, 1872*, 213; "Hannis Taylor," *Memorial Record of Alabama*, II, 600.

6. Richard V. Taylor, "Voice from Alabama," ch. 1, pp. 13–15.

7. Ibid.

8. Ibid.; Lela Legaré to Tennant S. McWilliams, February 17, 1972 in possession of the author.

9. Richard V. Taylor, "Voice from Alabama," ch. 1, pp. 13–15; Mary L. Taylor Hunt to Tennant S. McWilliams, January 21, 1972 in Hunt-McWilliams Correspondence.

10. Richard V. Taylor, "Voice from Alabama," ch. 1, p. 14; Hannis Taylor to Peter Alba, December 20, 1914, included in Erwin Craighead, *Mobile: Fact and Tradition* (Mobile: Powers Printing Co., 1913), 296–98; Oliver, "Centennial Commemoration of New Bern Academy," 4.

11. Alabama Supreme Court Roll of Attorneys and Solicitors (Alabama Supreme Court Library, Judicial Building, Montgomery, Alabama); Minutes of the Alabama Supreme Court, 1871–1872, p. 347 (Alabama Supreme Court Library, Judicial Building, Montgomery, Alabama); Oliver, "Centennial Commemoration of New Bern Academy," 4.

12. "Hannis Taylor," *NCAB*, 118; Owen, *History of Alabama*, IV, 1649; Commissions of Baldwin County, 1862–1882, p. 3 (Alabama State Department of Archives and History, Montgomery, Alabama); Mobile *Register*, April 7, 1893.

13. Owen, *History of Alabama*, III, 675; Mary L. Taylor Hunt to Tennant S. McWilliams, April 1, 1916 in Hunt-McWilliams Correspondence; *Mobile City Directory, 1873*, 75, 199.

14. The case was titled *William G. Strebling v. President of the Bank of Kentucky*. Clerk's Docket of the Alabama Supreme Court, January term 1872, p. 187 (Alabama Supreme Court Library, Judicial Building, Montgomery, Alabama); 48 *Alabama Reports* 451–54 (1872); Owen, *History of Alabama*, III, 675; Henry G. Connor, *John Archibald Campbell* (Boston: Houghton Mifflin Co., 1920), 256. Other significant cases which Taylor and Goldthwaite argued before the Alabama Supreme Court include *John L. Rapier, et al. v. Louisiana Equitable Life Insurance Company*, 57 *Alabama Reports* 100–04 (1876); and *Theodore J. Jones v. Sara Taylor*, 52 *Alabama Reports* 518–19 (1874).

15. Richard V. Taylor, "Voice from Alabama," ch. 1, pp. 13–15, ch. 2, pp. 1–3.

16. Ibid., ch. 2, p. 1, ch. 3, pp. 2–4; Spencer, "Chapel Hill, North Carolina Commencement, 1892"; Mary L. Taylor Hunt to Tennant S. McWilliams, April 1, 1969 in Hunt-McWilliams Correspondence.

17. Regina Rapier Marston to Tennant S. McWilliams, March 24, 1972 in possession of the author; Owen, *History of Alabama*, IV, 1413; Erwin Craighead, *From Mobile's Past* (Mobile: Powers Printing Co., 1925), 203–07; Charles G. Summersell, *Mobile: History of a Seaport Town* (University, Ala.: University of Alabama Press, 1949), 27–37, 45–47.

18. Regina Rapier Marston to Tennant S. McWilliams, March 24, 1972 in possession of the author; Palmer Pillans to Tennant S. McWilliams, Febraury 29, 1972 in posession of the author; Mobile *Register*, December 28, 1922, September 17, 1895, April 8, 1893; Hunt, "Memoirs," 9; Caldwell Delaney to Tennant S. McWilliams, July 17, 1972 in possession of the author; Thomas Cooper DeLeon, *Bienville Year Bicentennary: Mobile Carnival, 200 Years Between 1711 and 1911* ([n.p., 1911?]), 14.

19. Catholics held positions of prominence in Mobile partially because of the strong Catholic tradition in this Gulf region, which once was part of the Spanish and French empires. Interview with Monsignor Oscar H. Lipscomb, Chancellor of the Cathedral-Basilica of the Immaculate Conception, Mobile, Alabama, February 25, 2972.

20. Mary L. Taylor Hunt to Tennant S. McWilliams, September 8, 1966 in Hunt-McWilliams Correspondence.

21. Taylor encouraged Ryan to collect and publish the poems, and he also provided the *Register* with a laudatory review of Ryan's first volume when it appeared in 1879. He later oversaw the creation of a life-sized statue of the priest, which was placed in Ryan's Square at Mobile. Regina Rapier Marston to Tennant S. McWilliams, March 24, 1972 in possession of the author; Hannis Taylor, "Abram J. Ryan," *Library of Southern Literature* (17 vols., Atlanta: Martin and Hoyt Co., 1909–1913), X, 4625; Mobile *Register*, December 14, 1879, December 28, 1922; Craighead, *Mobile: Fact and Tradition*, 233–34; Rev. Oscar H. Lipscomb, "Some Unpublished Poems of Abram J. Ryan," *Alabama Review*, XXV (July 1972), 167.

22. Hannis Taylor, "Abram J. Ryan," *Library of Southern Literature*, X, 4625; Mary L. Taylor Hunt to Tennant S. McWilliams, January 21, 1972 in Hunt-McWilliams Correspondence.

23. Hannis Taylor to Cornelia Phillips Spencer, October 2, 1880 in Spencer Papers.

24. Mary L. Taylor Hunt to Tennant S. McWilliams, January 1, 1972 in Hunt-McWilliams Correspondence.

25. James B. Randall, "Sketch of our New Minister to Spain," *Church News*, reprinted in Mobile *Register*, June 11, 1893; Mobile *Register*, July 24, 1896; Mary L. Taylor Hunt to Tennant S. McWilliams, April 1, 1969 in Hunt-McWilliams Correspondence; Owen, *History of Alabama*, III, 622.

26. Hunt, "Memoirs," 2.

27. Owen, *History of Alabama*, IV, 1650.

28. Richard V. Taylor, "Voice from Alabama," ch. 1, p. 1, ch. 3, p. 4.

29. Hamilton, *Mobile of the Five Flags*, 365, 386–87; Mobile *Register*, August 23–25, November 10, 1878, January 15, 1879.

30. Mobile *Register*, November 17, 1878, February 15, 1881, April 7, 1893; "Hannis Taylor," *NCAB*, 113.

31. Mobile *Register*, December 6, 1878, January 12, 21, 1879.

32. Ibid., September 10, 1878, January 15, 16, 21, 23, 1879, February 15, 1881.

33. Ibid., February 12–18, March 12–18, 1879. Taylor's solution to the Mobile debt problem represents a strange blend of opposite political philosophies then taking hold in the South, retrenchment and readjustment. Mobile's reaction to readjustment, however, was in contrast to trends across the South, where wealth and power opposed Readjusters and supported Funders. C. Vann Woodward, *Origins of the New South* (Baton Rouge: Louisiana State University Press, 1951), 85–98.

34. Craighead, *Mobile: Fact and Tradition*, 132; Hamilton, *Mobile of the Five Flags*, 386–87.

35. Hannis Taylor to Cornelia Phillips Spencer, October 2, 1880 in Spencer Papers.

36. Owen, *History of Alabama*, III, 675; *Mobile City Directory, 1878*, 191.

37. See *The Union National Bank v. Julian S. Hartwell*, 84 *Alabama Reports*, 379–83 (1887); *Gulf City Paper Company v. John L. Rapier*, 77 *Alabama Reports* 126–37 (1876); and *Mobile and Ohio Railroad Company v. J. S. Nichols*, 98 *Alabama Reports* 92–129 (1892). This evaluation of Taylor's success as an attorney is based on an examination of the Clerk's Docket of the Alabama Supreme Court (Alabama Supreme Court Library, Judicial Building, Montgomery, Alabama) and decisions presented in *Alabama Reports*.

38. *Attorney Rolls of the United States Supreme Court: List of Attorneys and Counsellors Admitted to Practice in the Supreme Court of the United States*, 1790— 1886 (Washington: National Archives Microfilm Publications, 1955), Microcopy 217, roll 1, p. 223; *United States Supreme Court Minutes* (Washington: National Archives Microfilm Publication, 1954), Microcopy 215, roll 16.

39. *Port of Mobile v. Watson*, 116 *United States Reports* 289–306 (1885). Taylor was assisted in this case by John L. Smith and J. M. Johnston. United States Supreme Court Docket "U" (Washington: National Archives Micro-

film Publications, 1954), Microcopy 216, rolls 6 and 7; Mobile *Register*, February 15, 1881.

40. Hannis Taylor to Cornelia Phillips Spencer, August 8, 1889 in Spencer Papers.

41. Hannis Taylor to John Tyler Morgan, March 26, 1886 in John Tyler Morgan Papers (Manuscripts Division, Library of Congress, Washington, D.C.).

42. *Proceedings of the Alabama Bar Association, 1923* (Montgomery: Paragon Press, 1923), 316-17.

43. Ibid., 312-15; *Proceedings of the Alabama Bar Association, 1891* (Montgomery: Paragon Press, 1891), 53-64; Mobile *Register*, January 31, August 8, 18, 1890, July 9, 10, 1891, December 29, 1922; Hannis Taylor, *Origin and Growth of the English Constitution* (2 vols., Boston: Houghton Mifflin Co., 1889, 1898), I, passim.

44. *Ex parte Rapier*, 143 *United States Reports* 110-35 (1892). This case was heard simultaneously with *In re Dupre*, originated by the Louisiana State Lottery Company. Mobile *Register*, February 2, 1892; *Raleigh News and Observer*, February 2, 1892; *New York Times*, February 2, 1892; "Hannis Taylor," *NCAB*, 118.

45. 26 *United States Statutes at Large* 465 (1890). For background on the statute and its applicability to the Louisiana State Lottery, see John S. Ezell, *Fortune's Merry Wheel: The Lottery in America* (Cambridge: Harvard University Press, 1960), 237-46.

46. Mobile *Register*, October 7, November 25, 1890, March 5, April 28, 1891. Regardless of his attitude toward the constitutionality of the antilottery law, Rapier viewed lotteries as social evils and editorialized against them even while his case was in litigation. For example, see Mobile *Register*, August 12, 1890, November 14, December 4, 1891.

47. *Washington Post*, November 17, 1891; *New York Times*, November 17, 1891; Mobile *Register*, November 17, 1891; *Ex parte Rapier*, 143 *United States Reports* 110-35 (1892). Taylor's complete brief is published as *The Freedom of the Press in the Supreme Court of the United States. Argument of Hannis Taylor* (Washington: Judd Publishing Co., [1892]).

48. *Ex parte Rapier*, 143 *Lawyer's Edition* 93-103 (1892). During the 1890s the court employed the concept of due process in order to strike down reform legislation; the Rapier decision stands as a notable exception to this trend. Alfred H. Kelly and Winfred H. Harbison, *The American Constitution: Its Origin and Development* (4th ed., New York: W. W. Norton & Co., 1970), 500-46; Paul F. Boller, *American Thought in Transition: The Impact of Evolutionary Naturalism, 1865-1900* (Chicago: Rand McNally & Co., 1969), 168-73; Benjamin R. Twiss, *Lawyers and the Constitution: How Laissez-faire Came to*

the Supreme Court [1875–1935] (New York: Russell & Russell Publishers, 1962), 160–79.

49. *Washington Post*, November 18, 1891, February 3, 1892; Mobile *Register*, May 6, November 11, 1891, February 12, 1892.

50. Hannis Taylor, "A Blow at the Freedom of the Press," *North American Review*, CLV (December 1892), 694–705. Even before he heard the decision Taylor exhibited a strong sensitivity toward losing the case. "If the Court shall sustain the act as valid," he wrote Herbert Baxter Adams, "it will be the most dangerous principle recognized since the Civil War." Hannis Taylor to Herbert Baxter Adams, November 27, 1891 in Herbert Baxter Adams Papers (Milton S. Eisenhower Library, John Hopkins University, Baltimore, Maryland).

51. Hannis Taylor, "Independence of the Federal Judiciary," *American Law Review*, XL (July–August 1906), 494–95; Taylor, *Origin and Growth of the American Constitution*, 230–31; Mary L. Taylor Hunt to Tennant S. McWilliams, December 18, 1968 in Hunt-McWilliams Correspondence; Hannis Taylor, *Jurisdiction and Procedure of the Supreme Court of the United States* (Rochester: Lawyers' Co-operative Publishing Co., 1905), lvi, 495.

52. Interview with Mary L. Taylor Hunt, Boston, December 28, 1971; Mobile *Register*, November 24, 1891, August 11, October 2, 1892.

53. Hunt, "Memoirs," 1; Baptismal Records of St. Joseph's Church (Rectory, St. Joseph's Church, Mobile, Alabama).

54. Hunt, "Memoirs," 9; Mary L. Taylor Hunt to Tennant S. McWilliams, January 21, 1972 in Hunt-McWilliams Correspondence.

55. Interview with Mary L. Taylor Hunt, Boston, December 28, 1971; Hunt, "Memoirs," 5, 8, 17.

56. Hunt, "Memoirs," 6.

57. Ibid.; interview with Mrs. J. Lloyd Abbot, Mobile, Alabama, February 24, 1972.

58. Ibid.

59. Hannis Taylor to Peter Alba, December 20, 1914, in Craighead, *Mobile: Fact and Tradition*, 296, 298; Mobile *Register*, January 25, 1893; Mary L. Taylor Hunt to Tennant S. McWilliams, April 1, 1969 in Hunt-McWilliams Correspondence. For sketches of Alba, Croom, and Russell, see Owen, *History of Alabama*, III, 430, and IV, 1478; Craighead, *Mobile: Fact and Tradition*, 291–98.

60. Interview with Mary L. Taylor Hunt, Boston, December 28, 1971; Mary L. Taylor Hunt to Tennant S. McWilliams, March 21, 1972 in Hunt-McWilliams Correspondence; Regina Marston Rapier to Tennant S. McWilliams, March 24, 1972 in possession of the author; Beverly, "Hannis Taylor," 1.

61. T. Herndon Smith to Tennant S. McWilliams, March 3, 1972 in possession of the author.

62. Some of the publicists of the New South purposely glorified the old order so as to gain the support of wealthy and powerful leaders of the Old South. There is no indication that Taylor was so pragmatic. For an analysis of the New South movement, see Paul M. Gaston, *The New South Creed: A Study in Southern Mythmaking* (New York: Afred A. Knopf, 1970).

63. Hannis Taylor to John Tyler Morgan, February 23, 1887 in Matt W. Ransom Papers (Southern Historical Collection, University of North Carolina, Chapel Hill, North Carolina); Taylor, "A Political History of the State, 65, 93; Hannis Taylor, "Alabama," in *Encyclopaedia Britannica* (10th ed., 26 vols., Edinburgh: Britannica Co., 1902–1903), I, 237–38; Mobile *Register*, March 4, 1900.

64. *Congressional Record*, 49th Cong., 2nd Sess., 2522–23; Hannis Taylor to John Tyler Morgan, February 23, 1887 in Ransom Papers; Taylor, "Alabama," 238.

65. Woodward, *Origins of the New South*, 125; Summersell, *Mobile: History of a Seaport Town*, 47; Erwin C. Faile, "Thomas Greene Bush: Alabama Spokesman of the New South" (M.A. thesis, Auburn University, 1967), 45–49.

66. Taylor, "Political History of the State," 66–67.

67. Ibid., 71–80, 82, 94.

68. Boller, *American Thought in Transition*, 199–226; George M. Frederickson, *The Black Image in the White Mind: The Debate on Afro-American Character and Destiny* (New York: Harper & Row, Publishers, 1971), 228–55; Rubin Frances Weston, *Racism in U.S. Imperialism: The Influences of Racial Assumptions on American Foreign Policy, 1893–1946* (Columbia: University of South Carolina Press, 1972, passim.; John S. Haller, *Outcasts from Evolution: Scientific Attitudes of Racial Inferiority, 1859–1900* (Urbana: University of Illinois Press, 1971), passim.

69. Hannis Taylor to John Randolph Tucker, February 5, 1889 in Tucker Family Papers (Southern Historical Collection, University of North Carolina, Chapel Hill, North Carolina); Taylor, *Origin and Growth of the English Constitution*, I, Introduction.

70. Hannis Taylor to Kemp R. Battle, August 3, 1889 in Battle Family Papers (Southern Historical Collection, University of North Carolina, Chapel Hill, North Carolina); Hannis Taylor to John Randolph Tucker, February 5, 1889 in Tucker Family Papers; Hannis Taylor to Cornelia Phillips Spencer, July 6, 1889 in Spencer Papers; Mobile *Register*, December 28, 1922; Mary L. Taylor Hunt to Tennant S. McWilliams, August 17, 1966 in Hunt-McWilliams Correspondence.

71. Hannis Taylor to Herbert Baxter Adams, May 26, 1888 in Adams Papers; *Historical Scholarship in the United States, 1876–1901*, edited by W. S. Holt. The Johns Hopkins University Studies in History and Political Science, Series LVI, No. 4 (Baltimore: Johns Hopkins University Press, 1938), 113–15.

72. Hunt, "Memoirs," 19.

73. Hannis Taylor to [Henry C. Semple], January 31, 1889 in Tucker Family Papers; John Fiske to Hannis Taylor, [May ?], 1888, copy in Hannis Taylor to Cornelia Phillips Spencer, July 6, 1889 in Spencer Papers; John Fiske to James G. Blaine, March 22, 1892 in Recommendations and Applications for Office: Hannis Taylor (Civil Archives Division, National Archives, Washington, D.C.); John Fiske, "An American History of the English Constitution," *Atlantic Monthly*, LXV (February 1890), 263–66.

74. Edward A. Freeman to Hannis Taylor, May 30, 1888, copy in Hannis Taylor to Cornelia Phillips Spencer, July 6, 1889 in Spencer Papers; Mobile *Register*, November 16, 1898; Hannis Taylor, "Edward A. Freeman," *Yale Review*, II (August 1893), 159–72.

75. Hannis Taylor to Herbert Baxter Adams, May 7, 26, 1888, November 27, 1891 in Adams Papers. Others who assisted and encouraged Taylor include Professor John Randolph Tucker of Washington and Lee University, John Tyler Morgan, and Cornelia Phillips Spencer. Hannis Taylor to John Randolph Tucker, February 5, March 27, May 6, 1889 in Tucker Family Papers; Hannis Taylor to Cornelia Phillips Spencer, July 6, August 8, 1889 in Spencer Papers; Hannis Taylor to John Tyler Morgan, February 1, 1887 in Morgan Papers; Hannis Taylor to John Tyler Morgan, February 16, 23, 1887 in Ransom Papers.

76. Hannis Taylor to [Henry C. Semple], January 31, 1889 in Tucker Papers; John Fiske to Hannis Taylor, [May ?] 1888, copy in Hannis Taylor to Cornelia Phillips Spencer, July 6, 1889 in Spencer Papers.

77. *Washington Post*, April 7, 1893; *New York Times*, May 19, 1890; Mobile *Register*, August 31, November 2, 1890, February 17, November 11, 1891; John L. Stewart, Review of *Origin and Growth of the English Constitution*, in *Annals of the American Academy of Political and Social Science*, I (July 1890), 145–47; William P. Trent, "Notes on Recent Work in Southern History," *Proceedings of the Virginia Historical Society*, XI (December 1891), 56; Earl of Meath, "Anglo-Saxon Unity," *Fortnightly Review*, CCLXXXIX (April 1891), 615–22; Wendell Holmes Stephenson, *Southern History in the Making* (Baton Rouge: Louisiana State University Press, 1964), 132–33; W. C. Jackson, "Culture and the New Era in North Carolina," *North Carolina Historical Review*, II (January 1925), 16; *Transactions of the Alabama Historical Society*, *1898–1899*, ed. by Thomas M. Owen (4 vols., Tuscaloosa: Paragon Printers,

1899), IV, 20, 195–97, 200; Summersell, *Mobile: History of a Seaport Town*, 54–55.

78. William A. Dunning, Review of *Origin and Growth of the English Constitution*, in *Political Science Quarterly*, V (March 1890), 188–90.

79. Hannis Taylor to Herbert Baxter Adams, May 15, 1890 in Adams Papers; Hannis Taylor to Cornelia Phillips Spencer, July 6, August 8, 1889 in Spencer Papers; Hannis Taylor to John Randolph Tucker, February 5, 1889 in Tucker Papers.

80. Mrs. Alexander Foreman, "Hospitals of Mobile," 3 (typed MS in Manuscripts Collection, Museum of the City of Mobile, Mobile, Alabama).

81. *Alabama Senate Journal, 1890–1* (Montgomery: Brown Printing Co., 1891), 212; Mobile *Register*, January 24, 25, February 3, 1891; "Hannis Taylor," *Memorial Record of Alabama*, II, 600; Going, *Bourbon Democracy in Alabama*, 138–39; Willis Gaylord Clark, *A History of Education in Alabama*, Bureau of Education, Circular of Information, No. 163 (Washington: Government Printing Office, 1889), 147–52.

82. *Acts of the General Assembly of Alabama, 1890–91* (Montgomery: Roemer Printing Co., 1891), 759.

83. Taylor also served as a social member of the Manasas Club, his wife as a member of the Colonial Dames, and together they participated in balls and parades of the First Regiment of the Alabama State Troops. Mobile *Register*, February 14, 1892, April 9, 1899; Hannis Taylor to Peter Alba, December 20, 1914 in Craighead, *Mobile: Fact and Tradition*, 296–98.

84. In writing about Reconstruction, William A. Dunning criticized political motivations of the Republican party and defended the efforts of Southern whites to resurrect their antebellum society. Michael Kraus, *The Writing of American History* (Norman: University of Oklahoma Press, 1953), 305–07.

85. Taylor, "Political History of the State," 86–94.

86. Ibid., 87, 94; Taylor, "Alabama," *Encyclopaedia Britannica*, 237–39.

87. Mobile *Register*, April 6, 16, May 1, 6, 1879.

88. Hannis Taylor, "The Speaker's Tyranny," *New York Times*, November 19, 1890; Mobile *Register*, November 26, 1890; "Hannis Taylor," *Memorial Record of Alabama*, II, 600.

89. The Blair Bill, introduced into the United States Senate in 1883, called for ten annual education appropriations beginning at $15,000,000 and decreasing by $1,000,000 each year. Since the funds would be distributed to the states on the basis of illiteracy rates, Southern states would be the major beneficiaries of the proposal. Allen J. Going, "The South and the Blair Bill," *Mississippi Valley Historical Review*, XLIV (September 1957), 267–90.

90. Hannis Taylor to John Tyler Morgan, March 26, 1886 in Morgan Papers.

91. Ibid.; August C. Radke, "John Tyler Morgan, Expansionist Senator, 1877–1907" (Ph.D dissertation, University of Washington, 1954), 79, 90–91; Going, *Bourbon Democracy in Alabama*, 156–57.

Chapter III

1. Peter J. Hamilton to Thomas Goode Jones, March 4, 1891 in Thomas Goode Jones Papers (Manuscripts Division, Alabama State Department of Archives and History, Montgomery, Alabama); Mobile *Register*, February 17, 21, 24, 27, March 1, 5, 1891.

2. John Tyler Morgan to James G. Blaine, January 12, 1892; William C. Oates to James G. Blaine, January 25, 1892; John Fiske to James G. Blaine, March 22, 1892 in Applications and Recommendations for Office: Hannis Taylor (Civil Archives Division, National Archives, Washington, D.C.); Hannis Taylor to John Tyler Morgan, January 20, 1892 in Morgan Papers; Raleigh *News and Observer*, April 7, 1893; Mobile *Register*, April 7, May 7, 1893.

3. Those who helped Taylor obtain the appointment include these leaders of the Democratic party in Alabama: John Tyler Morgan, Edward L. Russell, Charles M. Shelley, James L. Pugh, William C. Oates, Joseph H. Wheeler, John H. Bankhead, and Richard H. Clarke. J. L. M. Curry to Grover Cleveland, March 17, 1893; E. L. Russell to Grover Cleveland, March 11, 1893; C. M. Shelley to Grover Cleveland, March 5, 1893; James L. Pugh to Grover Cleveland, March 17, 1893; William C. Oates to Grover Cleveland, March 6, 1893 in Nathaniel H. R. Dawson Papers (Southern Historical Collection, University of North Carolina, Chapel Hill, North Carolina); Hannis Taylor to Joseph H. Wheeler, February 25, 1893 in Joseph H. Wheeler Papers (Manuscripts Division, Alabama State Department of Archives and History, Montgomery, Alabama); Mobile *Register*, April 12, 1893; *Washington Post*, April 7, 1893; *Congressional Record*, 53rd Cong., 1st Sess. (1893), pt. 1, 100, 134. For the political context of Taylor's appointment see Dewey W. Grantham, *Hoke Smith and the Politics of the New South* (Baton Rouge: Louisiana State University Press, 1958), 62.

4. *Register of the Department of State* (Washington: Government Printing Office, 1897), 17; Hannis Taylor to Walter Q. Gresham, April 18, 1893 in U.S. Department of State, Spain: Despatches. CXII–CXXXI (April 18, 1893–September 29, 1897). Hereafter cited as Spain: Despatches. Microfilm copies of Taylor's official correspondence, unless otherwise noted, are found in National Archives Microfilm Publications, Microcopy No. 31, rolls 118–22. Hannis Taylor to Richard Olney, No. 505, May 1, 1896, ibid.; Hunt,

"Memoirs," 11; Hannis Taylor to Cornelia Phillips Spencer, December 25, 1894 in Spencer Papers; Mobile *Register*, April 8, 16, 1893, January 18, 1895.

5. Hannis Taylor to W. Q. Gresham, April 27, 1893 and No. 267, December 7, 1894 in Spain: Despatches; Hunt, "Memoirs," 10; Mobile *Register*, May 14, 19, 25, June 7, 11, 1893.

6. Hunt, "Memoirs," 10-16.

7. Ibid.

8. Ibid.

9. James C. Carter to Grover Cleveland, February 25, 1893 in Applications and Recommendations for Office: Hannis Taylor; Hannis Taylor to W. Q. Gresham, No. 2, July 3, 1893, No. 3, July 3, 1893, No. 36, September 15, 1893, No. 130, February 22, 1894 in Spain: Despatches; Mobile *Register*, December 3, 1893.

10. Raymond Carr, *Spain 1808-1939* (Oxford: The Clarendon Press, 1966), 347-78; Gerald Brenan, *The Spanish Labyrinth* (New York: Macmillan, Co., 1943), passim; Ernest May, *Imperial Democracy: The Emergence of America as a World Power* (New York: Harcourt, Brace & World, 1961), 94-111.

11. For background on the Mora claim see U.S. Department of State, *Foreign Relations, 1893-1894* (Washington: Government Printing Office, 1895), Appendix I, 364-412; Hannis Taylor to W. Q. Gresham, No. 137, March 15, 1894, and No. 377, June 20, 1895 in Spain: Despatches.

12. Hannis Taylor to W. Q. Gresham, No. 72, November 24, 1893, No. 90, December 23, 1893 in Spain: Despathces.

13. Hannis Taylor to W. Q. Gresham, No. 91, December 25, 1893, No. 94, December 30, 1893, No. 97, January 4, 1894 in Spain: Despatches.

14. Hannis Taylor to W. Q. Gresham, No. 128, February 17, 1894, No. 135, March 2, 1894, No. 137, March 5, 1894, No. 149, March 19, 1894, No. 282, January 4, 1895 in Spain: Despatches; E. F. Uhl to Hannis Taylor, No. 142, June 13, 1894 in U.S. Department of State, Spain: Instructions, XXI-XXII (March 9, 1891-March 9, 1900). Hereafter cited as Spain: Instructions. Microfilm copies of these instructions are included in National Archives Microfilm Publications, Microcopy 77, rolls 149-150.

15. Henry James, *Richard Olney and His Public Service* (Boston: Houghton Mifflin Co. 1923), 152-63; U.S. Department of State, *Foreign Relations, 1895* (Washington: Government Printing Office, 1896), 1174-76; French Ensor Chadwick, *The Relations of the United States With Spain: Diplomacy* (New York: Charles Scribner's Sons, 1909), 425; Hannis Taylor to Richard Olney, No. 377, June 20, 1895, No. 394, July 10, 1895 in Spain: Despatches; A. A. Adee to Hannis Taylor, No. 364, July 9, 1895, and telegram, August 12, 1895 in Spain: Instructions.

16. The Carolines claim is introduced in Julius W. Pratt, *The Expansionists of 1898: The Acquisition of Hawaii and the Spanish Islands* (Baltimore: Johns Hopkins University Press, 1936), 290, 302–04. Also see *Foreign Relations, 1893–94*, 559–62; Pearle E. Quinn, "The Diplomatic Struggle for the Carolines, 1898," *Pacific Historical Review*, XIV (September 1945), 290–92.

17. Hannis Taylor to W. Q. Gresham, No. 33, August 19, 1893, in Spain: Despatches.

18. For example see Hannis Taylor to W. Q. Gresham, No. 43, October 14, 1893, No. 113, January 24, 1894, No. 145, March 16, 1894, in Spain: Despatches; A. A. Adee to Hannis Taylor, No. 35, September 22, 1893, Edwin F. Uhl to Hannis Taylor, No. 115, April 28, 1894 in Spain: Instructions.

19. Hannis Taylor to W. Q. Gresham, No. 145, March 16, 1894, No. 157, April 16, 1894, No. 164, May 11, 1894 in Spain: Despatches.

20. Hannis Taylor to W. Q. Gresham, No. 113, January 24, 1894, No. 162, May 4, 1894, No. 163, May 7, 1894, No. 167, May 14, 1894 in Spain: Despatches.

21. Hannis Taylor to W. Q. Gresham, No. 176, June 4, 1894, No. 187, June 7, 1897, No. 193, June 22, 1894, No. 209, July 13, 1894 in Spain: Despatches; Quinn, "Diplomatic Struggle for the Carolines," 292.

22. Richard Olney to Hannis Taylor, No. 425, November 7, 1895 in Spain: Instructions; Hannis Taylor to Richard Olney, No. 473, January 21, 1896 in Spain: Despatches; Quinn, "Diplomatic Struggle for the Carolines," 293–302.

23. There are numerous studies on American reactions to the Cuban revolution and the origins of the Spanish-American War. One of the most detailed accounts is Chadwick, *Relations of the United States With Spain*, 387–572. A more recent interpretive treatment that contains excellent bibliographical notes is H. Wayne Morgan, *America's Road to Empire: The War With Spain and Overseas Expansion* (New York: John Wiley & Sons, 1965).

24. For background on the *Alliança* affair see Chadwick, *Relations of the United States With Spain*, 419–20.

25. W. Q. Gresham to Hannis Taylor, March 14, 1895 in Spain: Instructions; Hannis Taylor to W. Q. Gresham, No. 318, March 6, 1895, Duke of Tetuan to Hannis Taylor, April 9, 1895, enclosed in Hannis Taylor to W. Q. Gresham, No. 336, April 13, 1895 in Spain: Despatches.

26. May, *Imperial Democracy*, 83–84; W. Q. Gresham to Hannis Taylor, telegram, April 16, 1895 in Spain: Instructions; Hannis Taylor to W. Q. Gresham, No. 344, April 20, 1895, No. 357, May 20, 1895 in Spain: Despatches; Mobile *Register*, April 25, 1895.

27. May, *Imperial Democracy*, 88; Hannis Taylor to Cornelia Phillips Spencer, October 27, 1895 in Spencer Papers; Hannis Taylor to Gaylord B. Clark, October 17, 1895 in Hannis Taylor Correspondence (in possession of Mrs. Gossett McRae, Mobile, Alabama); Mobile *Register*, October 24, 1895. See also Stephen Bonsal to W. Q. Gresham, October 5, 1893, Hannis Taylor to W. Q. Gresham, No. 66, November 11, 1893, No. 342, April 18, 1895, and H. Clay Armstrong to Richard Olney, No. 414, September 6, 1895 in Spain: Despatches.

28. New Orleans *Times-Democrat*, August 28, 1895; Richard Olney to Hannis Taylor, November 14, 1895 in Richard Olney Papers (Manuscripts Division, Library of Congress, Washington, D.C.); Richard Olney to Grover Cleveland, November 6, 13, 1895 in Grover Cleveland Papers (Manuscripts Division, Library of Congress, Washington, D.C.).

29. *A Compilation of the Messages and Papers of Presidents*, edited by James D. Richardson (20 vols., New York: Bureau of National Literature, 1897–1917), XIII, 6068.

30. Hannis Taylor to Henry Cabot Lodge, June 27, 1895 in Henry Cabot Lodge Papers (Manuscripts Division, Massachusetts Historical Society, Boston, Massachusetts); Henry Cabot Lodge to Theodore Roosevelt, October 13, 23, 1895 in *Selections from the Correspondence of Theodore Roosevelt and Henry Cabot Lodge*, ed. by Allan Nevins (2 vols., New York: Macmillan Co., 1933), I, 187, 194; Hannis Taylor, "Review of the Cuban Question in Its Economic, Political, and Diplomatic Aspects," *North American Review*, CLXV (November 1897), 610–35; Hannis Taylor to Cornelia Phillips Spencer, October 27, 1895 in Spencer Papers; May, *Imperial Democracy*, 99–100; Mobile *Register*, April 20, 1899.

31. Richard Olney to Hannis Taylor, December 13, 1895 in Olney Papers; Hunt, "Memoirs," 14. After this run-in with Olney, it took blind gall for Taylor to apply for the post of minister to Russia, which would have been a promotion. He did not get the job. See Hannis Taylor to Joseph Wheeler, January 29, 1896 in Joseph Wheeler Papers.

32. *Washington Post*, February 20, 1896; Raleigh *News and Observer*, February 20, 1896.

33. For background on the *Competitor* affair see Chadwick, *Relations of the United States With Spain*, 468–71.

34. Richard Olney to Hannis Taylor, telegram, May 1, 9, 1896 in Spain: Instructions; Hannis Taylor to Richard Olney, telegram, May 4, 1896, No. 510, May 11, 1896, and telegram, September 6, 1896 in Spain: Despatches; Mobile *Register*, May 10, 12, 1896; May, *Imperial Democracy*, 84. When Taylor returned to the United States in 1897, he published an article explaining

Spain's political decadence and its inability to resolve the Cuban problem. Infuriated over the article, Spanish officials announced that they regretted having released the *Competitor* crew. See Taylor, "Review of the Cuban Question," 610–35; *New York Times*, November 5, 1897.

35. Richard Olney to Hannis Taylor, "personal," February 25, 1897 in Spain: Instructions; Hannis Taylor to [Charles LeBaron Taylor], August 25, 1896 in Hannis Taylor Correspondence; Hannis Taylor to Richard Olney, "personal," February 4, 1897, and Hannis Taylor to John Sherman, No. 754, September 10, 1897 in Spain: Despatches; *Atlanta Constitution*, March 11, 1900; Boston *Journal*, April 20, 1899; Mobile *Register*, June 10, 12, 18, 1896; *New York Times*, September 22, October 10, 1897; Hunt, "Memoirs," 13, 16; Mary L. Taylor Hunt to Tennant S. McWilliams, June 18, August 17, 1966 in Hunt-McWilliams Correspondence; Thomas A. Bailey, *Diplomatic History of the American People* (8th ed., New York: Appleton-Century-Crofts, 1969), 452; Pratt, *Expansionists of 1898*, 210; interview with Mary L. Taylor Hunt, December 28, 1971.

36. *New York Times*, November 18, 1896; Mary L. Taylor Hunt to Tennant S. McWilliams, August 17, 1966 in Hunt-McWilliams Correspondence; Hannis Taylor to J. H. H. Peshine, September 6, 1897 in Records of the Foreign Service Posts of the Department of State; Spain—Miscellaneous Letters, XXXII (Civil Archives Division, National Archives, Washington, D.C.).

37. Orestes Ferrara, *The Last Spanish War* (New York: Paisley Press, 1937), 14–48; R. G. Neale, *Great Britain and U.S. Expansion 1898–1900* (Ann Arbor: University of Michigan Press, 1966, 11–12; Walter LaFeber, *The New Empire: An Interpretation of American Expansion, 1860–1898* (Ithaca, N.Y.: Cornell University Press, 1963), 284–95; May, *Imperial Democracy*, 109; Mary L. Taylor Hunt to Milo B. Howard, Jr., June 18, 1966 in Hunt-McWilliams Correspondence; Mobile *Register*, November 16, 1898.

38. Hannis Taylor to Richard Olney, No. 549, August 11, 1898, No. 551, August 13, 1896 in Spain: Despatches; London *Standard*, August 11, 1896; London *Times*, August 11, 1896; *New York Times*, August 11, 1896; New York *Journal*, January 11, 1897; Ferrara, *Last Spanish War*, 48–64.

39. Unidentified clipping in Hannis Taylor Correspondence; Hannis Taylor, "Pending Problems," *North American Review*, CLXVII (November 1898), 618; Ferrara, *Last Spanish War*, 63. As war was about to break out in 1898 Spain futilely tried again to align Europe against United States intervention. See May, *Imperial Democracy*, 196–219.

40. Hannis Taylor to Richard Olney, No. 556, October 5, 1898 in Spain: Despatches; Hannis Taylor to Gaylord B. Clark, September 30, 1896 in Hannis Taylor Correspondence.

41. *Messages and Papers of Presidents*, IX, 716–22; LaFeber, *New Empire*, 295–96.

42. New York *Journal*, January 11, 1897; Mobile *Register*, January 9, 13, 31, 1897; John A. S. Grenville and George Berkeley Young, *Politics, Strategy, and American Diplomacy: Studies in Foreign Policy, 1873–1917* (New Haven: Yale University Press, 1966), 247.

43. Hannis Taylor to John Sherman, No. 658, March 5, 1897, No. 683, April 21, 1897 in Spain: Despatches; Mobile *Register*, June 17, 1896, April 6, 1897; Raleigh *News and Observer*, November 19, 1896; Charles E. Dawes, *Journal of the McKinley Years* (Chicago: Lakeside Press, 1950), 120–22; Allan Nevins, *Henry White* (New York: Dodd, Mead & Co. 1937), 122; Morgan, *America's Road to Empire*, 23.

44. Hannis Taylor to John Sherman, No. 755, September 14, 1897 in Spain: Despatches; Hannis Taylor, "Work of the Peace Commission," *North American Review*, CLXVII (December 1898), 746; *Washington Post*, September 14, 1897.

45. Hunt, "Memoirs," 11; Mary L. Taylor Hunt to Tennant S. McWilliams, June 2, 14, 1972 in Hunt-McWilliams Correspondence; Taylor, "Work of the Peace Commission," 745–46; *Washington Star*, October 9, 1897; Mobile *Register*, November 16, 1898; *Atlanta Constitution*, November 29, 1897.

46. Grover Cleveland to Richard Olney, November 11, 1897 in *Letters of Grover Cleveland*, ed. by Allan Nevins (New York: Dodd, Mead & Co., 1932), 517–18; Richard Olney to Grover Cleveland, November 8, 1897, and Grover Cleveland to Richard Olney, January 23, 1898 in Grover Cleveland Papers.

47. H. Wayne Morgan to Tennant S. McWilliams, January 12, 1972 in possession of the author; H. Wayne Morgan, *William McKinley and His America* (Syracuse: Syracuse University Press, 1963), 337; Morgan, *America's Road to Empire*, 23.

48. Interview with Mary L. Taylor Hunt, Boston, December 28, 1971.

Chapter IV

1. New York *Tribune*, June 20, 1897; Mobile *Register*, June 18, 20, 1897.

2. O. Lawrence Burnette, Jr., "John Tyler Morgan and Expansionist Sentiment in the New South," *Alabama Review*, XVIII (July 1965), 180–81; John L. Offner, "President McKinley and the Origins of the Spanish-American War" (Ph.D. dissertation, Pennsylvania State University, 1957), 158; Hilary Herbert, "Grandfather Talks About His Life Under Two Flags," 311 in Hilary Herbert Papers (Southern Historical Collection, University of North Carolina, Chapel Hill, North Carolina); Gerald G. Eggert,

"Our Man in Havana: Fitzhugh Lee," *Hispanic American Historical Review*, XLVII (November 1967), 463–85; Mobile *Register*, October 26, November 30, 1897.

3. Taylor, "Work of the Peace Commission," 746; Hunt, "Memoirs," 14; Mobile *Register*, April 20, 1899.

4. See Hannis Taylor, "Review of the Cuban Question," 610–35.

5. Martha Ashley Girling, "Southern Attitudes Towards the Cuban Craze" (M.A. thesis, Mississippi State University, 1960), 10–15; George W. Auxier, "Propaganda Activities of the Cuban *Junta* in Precipitating the Spanish-American War, 1895–1898," *Hispanic American Historical Review*, XIX (August 1939), 300; "Ex-Minister Taylor on Cuba," *Nation*, LXV, (November 4, 1897), 350–51; *Atlanta Constitution*, March 11, 1900; *Boston Herald*, August 3, 1898; Raleigh *News and Observer*, November 6, 7, 1897; Mobile *Register*, November 4, 9, 13, 14, December 1, 1897, January 8, April 18, August 3, 1898, April 25, 1899.

6. William E. Chandler to Hannis Taylor, September 9, 1902 in Spain: Claims, 1901—Miscellaneous Correspondence of William E. Chandler Regarding the Spanish Treaty Claims Commission, 1901–1907 (Civil Archives Division, National Archives, Washington, D.C.); Horace Edgar Flack, *Spanish-American Relations Preceding the War of 1898* (Baltimore: Johns Hopkins University Press, 1906), 48–49; London *Times*, November 6, 1897; *Pall Mall Gazette*, November 6, 1897; *New York Times*, November 3, 4, 5, 7, 9, 1897; *Washington Post*, November 6, December 1897; New York *Evening Post*, reprinted in Mobile *Register*, November 5, 1897; Raleigh *News and Observer*, November 7, 1897; Mobile *Register*, November 7, December 3, 1897.

7. *Washington Post*, November 6, 1897; London *Times*, November 6, 1897; Grenville and Young, *Politics, Strategy, and American Diplomacy*, 247; LeFeber, *New Empire*, 341; May, *Imperial Democracy*, 145.

8. *New York Times*, November 7, 13, 1897; *Washington Post*, November 9, 1897; Chicago *Times-Herald*, reprinted in Mobile *Register*, November 9, 1897; Mobile *Register*, November 10, 1897.

9. New York *Tribune*, November 15, 1897; *New York Times*, November 20, 1897; *Washington Post*, November 20, 1897; Mobile *Register*, November 20, 1897.

10. Peter E. Hagan, *The Catholic University of America: The Rectorship of Thomas J. Conaty* (Washington, D.C.: Catholic University of America Press, 1949), 107–08; Mobile *Register*, November 26, 27, 30, 1897. For Taylor's later defense of the article see Mobile *Register*, November 16, 1898, April 20, 1899; Taylor, "Work of the Peace Commission," 746; Hannis Taylor, "Spain's Political Future," *North American Review*, CLXVI (June 1898), 686–87.

11. *Atlanta Constitution*, November 29, 1897; Mobile *Register*, November 28, 30, 1897.

12. Richard V. Taylor, "Voice from Alabama," ch. 4, pp. 6–8; Mary L. Taylor Hunt to Tennant S. McWilliams, January 21, 1972 in Hunt-McWilliams Correspondence; Hunt, "Memoirs," 14; interview with Mrs. J. Lloyd Abbot, Mobile, February 24, 1972; *Mobile City Directory 1898* through *1901*; Owen, *History of Alabama*, III, 33; *Washington Post*, December 22, 1922; Mobile *Register*, December 25, 1897, July 18, 1899, June 18, 1901.

13. Mobile *Register*, January 26, March 18, 1898, January 1, 1899, February 27, May 24, June 24, 1900.

14. Interview with Palmer Pillans, February 22, 1972; Mobile *Register*, January 22, 23, 1898.

15. *Messages and Papers of Presidents*, XIII, 6251–76; Morgan, *America's Road to Empire*, 34; Morgan, *William McKinley and His America*, 348; New York *Tribune*, December 8, 1897; *New York Times*, December 8, 1897; *Washington Post*, December 8, 1897; *Springfield* [Massachusetts] *Republican*, December 9, 1897; Mobile *Register*, December 8, 1897; Raleigh *News and Observer*, December 8, 1897; *Atlanta Constitution*, March 11, 1900.

16. Hannis Taylor, "Empire Never Waits," *The Illustrated American*, XXIII (January–June 1898), 8–9. Also see reprint in Mobile *Register*, January 2, 1898.

17. Mobile *Register*, February 13, 1893.

18. Morgan, *America's Road to Empire*, passim.; Robert L. Beisner, *Twelve Against Empire: The Anti-Imperialists, 1898–1900* (New York: McGraw-Hill Book Co., 1968), passim.

19. Battle, *History of the University of North Carolina*, II, 554; Hannis Taylor, "Our Widening Destiny," Commencement Address at the University of North Carolina, June 1898, printed in Raleigh *News and Observer*, June 1, 1898; Mobile *Register*, December 23, 1897, January 8, 27, April 15, 17, June 2, 4, 13, 1898.

20. Reacting to strong pressure from the United States, Cuba agreed to a "quasi-protectorate status" by incorporating the Platt Amendment into its new constitution. Bailey, *Diplomatic History*, 499.

21. Hannis Taylor, "Conquered Territory and the Constitution," *North American Review*, CLXXIII (November 1901), 577–93; Taylor, "Work of the Peace Commission," 749, 751; Mobile *Register*, April 20, 1899; St. Louis *Globe-Democrat*, November 11, 1898; *Washington Post*, February 2, 1899. Some Southerners opposed imperialism on racial grounds. For example see William F. Holmes, *The White Chief: James Kimble Vardaman* (Baton Rouge: Louisiana State University, 1970), 288–89; Frances B. Simkins, "Ben

Tillman's View of the Negro," *Journal of Southern History*, III (May 1937), 173; Christopher Lasch, "The Anti-Imperialists, the Philippines, and the Inequality of Man," *Journal of Southern History*, XIV (August 1958), 319–31. Other Southerners opposed imperialism out of fear of the increased power of big business and the self-corrupting nature of imperial government. See Joseph L. Morrison, *Josephus Daniels: Small-d Democrat* (Chapel Hill: University of North Carolina Press, 1966), 36; C. Vann Woodward, *Tom Watson: Agrarian Rebel* (New York: Oxford University Press, 1938), 334–35.

22. Taylor, "Conquered Territory and the Constitution," 586, 591; Taylor, "Pending Problems," 624; St. Louis *Globe-Democrat*, November 11, 1898. For his earlier examination of the subject see Hannis Taylor, "England's Colonial Empire," *North American Review*, CLXII (June 1896), 682–97.

23. Samuel C. Parke, "Causes of the Philippine War," *The Arena*, XXVII (June 1902), 567; Taylor, "Pending Problems," 619–23; Taylor, "Conquered Territory and the Constitution," 592ff; Boston *Journal*, April 20, 1899; St. Louis *Globe-Democrat*, November 11, 1898; Mobile *Register*, December 1, 1898; Hannis Taylor, "Is Colonization a Crime?," *North American Review*, CLXXXIII (October 1906), 743–44; Hannis Taylor, "The American Commonwealth and Its Relations to the East and West," reprinted in *Congressional Record*, 62nd Cong., 2nd Sess. (1912), 333–35. On America's China policy during this time, see Charles S. Campbell, *Special Business Interests and the Open Door Policy* (New Haven: Yale University Press, 1951), passim., and Jerry Israel, *Progressivism and the Open Door* (Pittsburgh: University of Pittsburgh Press, 1971), passim.

24. Burnette, "John Tyler Morgan and Expansionist Sentiment in the New South," passim.; Radke, "John Tyler Morgan," passim.; Norman H. Blake, "Background to Cleveland's Venezuelan Policy," *American Historical Review*, XLVIII (January 1942), 264; John P. Dyer, *"Fight'n" Joe Wheeler* (Baton Rouge: Louisiana State University Press, 1941), 327–66, 382–84; Joseph Wheeler, "Our Duty in the Venezuelan Affair," *North American Review*, CLXI (November 1895), 628–33. Although Southern political leaders as a whole appear to have voted against Republican expansionist measures, many noted representatives and senators from the South as well as journalists gave strong support to political and economic imperialism during the late nineteenth century. See Tennant S. McWilliams, "The Lure of Empire: Southern Interest in the Caribbean, 1877–1900," *Mississippi Quarterly*, XXIX (Winter 1975–76), 43–63; Edward W. Chester, *Sectionalism, Politics, and American Diplomacy* (Metuchen, N.J.: Scarecrow Press, 1975), passim.

25. *Clarke County* [Alabama]*Democrat*, February 17, 1898; Mobile *Register*, August 9, 1898; William Warren Rogers, *The One-Gallused Rebellion: Ag-*

rarianism in Alabama, 1865–1896 (Baton Rouge: Louisiana State University Press, 1970), 223–84, 315; Inez Perry Langham, "Politics in Mobile County, 1890–1900" (M.A. thesis, University of Alabama, 1947), passim. Charles Mohr, *Timber Pines of the Southern States*, United States Bureau of Agriculture, Division of Forestry, Bulletin No. 13 (Washington: Government Printing Office, 1896), 38–41, 61–62, 76.

26. Mary Margaret Flock, ed., *To Inquiring Friends—If Any: Autobiography of John McDuffie* (Mobile: Azalea Printers, 1969), 53; *Clarke County* [Alabama] *Democrat*, February 17, March 3, 1898; Mobile *Register*, January 23, 29, 1892, September 3, October 6, 1896, February 25, April 5, 8, 12, 26, August 18, 1898, September 18, 1900; *Biographical Directory of the American Congress* (Washington: Government Printing Office, 1971), 1793–94.

27. Hannis Taylor to Richard H. Clarke, January 11, 1898, printed in Mobile *Register* August 9, 1898; Flock, *To Inquiring Friends*, 53; interview with Palmer Pillans, February 22, 1972; *Boston Herald*, August 3, 1898.

28. *Clarke County* [Alabama] *Democrat*, February 17, March 3, 1898; Mobile *Register*, March 3, November 4, 1898.

29. David Mathews, Sr. to Tennant S. McWilliams, June 26, 1972 in possession of the author; Flock, *To Inquiring Friends*, 54; Hunt, "Memoirs," 8; Mary L. Taylor Hunt to Tennant S. McWilliams, April 1, 1969 in Hunt-McWilliams Correspondence; Mobile *Register*, March 17, 29, April 2, May 15, 17, June 19, 1898; *Clarke County* [Alabama] *Democrat*, March 24, 1898.

30. Interview with Mary L. Taylor Hunt, December 28, 1971; Mobile *Register*, July 21–23, 1898.

31. Mobile *Register*, July 21–23, 1898.

32. Ibid.

33. Mobile *Register*, August 7, 9, 12, 1898; Hannis Taylor to Joseph F. Johnston, August 27, 1898 in Joseph F. Johnston Governor's Papers (Manuscripts Division, Alabama State Department of Archives and History, Montgomery, Alabama).

34. Flock, *To Inquiring Friends*, 52–55; Mobile *Register*, August 12–27, September 6–14, 1898; Hannis Taylor to Joseph F. Johnson, August 14, 1898 in Joseph F. Johnston Governor's Papers.

35. Mobile *Register*, September 14–25, 1898. Choctaw County was the only portion of the district that sent a Populist delegation to the state House of Representatives during 1894 when Populists were strongest in Alabama. Sheldon Hackney, *Populism to Progressivism in Alabama* (Princeton: Princeton University Press, 1969), 343; Rogers, *One-Gallused Rebellion*, 135, 208, 223, 262, 306, 315, 284.

36. Mobile *Register*, September 16, 27, November 4, 6, 8, 9, 1898.

37. *Thomasville Argus*, March 30, 1899; Boston *Journal*, April 20, 1899;

Boston *Advertiser*, April 25, 1899; Mobile *Register*, November 5, 10, 1898, February 15, March 26, May 13, 16, 1899; Richard E. Welch, "Senator George Frisbie Hoar and the Defeat of Anti-Imperialism, 1898–1900," *Historian*, XXVI (May 1964), 362–80. With Frederick Bromberg, Peter Hamilton, and other Mobile leaders, Taylor made a much publicized though fruitless effort to obtain the appointment of Charles K. Holt as Register in the Chancery Court at Mobile. See Mobile *Register*, November 5–6, 1898, for example.

38. Jackson *South Alabamian*, reprinted in Mobile *Register*, April 3, 1898.

39. Hannis Taylor to Woodrow Wilson, January 7, 1913 in Woodrow Wilson Papers (Manuscripts Division, Library of Congress, Washington, D.C.); Mobile *Register*, July 11, 12, 1899; Louis W. Koenig, *Bryan: A Political Biography of William Jennings Bryan* (New York: G. P. Putnam's Sons, 1971), 271–93. Taylor's developing attitudes towards corporate regulation will be analyzed fully in Chapter V.

40. For example, see Mobile *Register*, April 15, May 31, August 14, 1900.

41. Hannis Taylor to Erwin Craighead, June 18, 1900 in Erwin Craighead Papers (in possession of Caldwell Delaney, Mobile, Alabama); unidentified clipping in Peter Joseph Hamilton Papers (Manuscripts Division, Alabama State Department of Archives and History, Montgomery, Alabama); Mobile *Register*, April 15, June 20, 1900.

42. David Mathews, Sr. to Tennant S. McWilliams, June 26, 1972 in possession of the author; Boston *Herald*, reprinted in Mobile *Register*, July 31, 1900; Montgomery *Journal*, June 22, 1900; Montgomery *Advertiser*, August 1, 1900; Birmingham *Age-Herald*, reprinted in Mobile *Register*, April 15, 1900; Jackson *South Alabamian*, July 7, 1900; Mobile *Register*, June 20, 26, July 10, 7, August 8, 1900.

43. Mobile *Register*, July 20, 27, 1900.

44. Alfred R. Taylor, "Reminiscenses [of Hannis Taylor]," 4–5 in Alfred R. Taylor Collection (Southern Historical Collection, University of North Carolina, Chapel Hill, North Carolina); *The Catholic Truth*, reprinted in Mobile *Register*, August 12, 1900; David Mathews, Sr. to Tennant S. McWilliams, July 26, 1972 in possession of the author; Hunt, "Memoirs," 8–9; Mary L. Taylor Hunt to Tennant S. McWilliams, April 4, 1969, January 21, 1972, June 14, 1972 in Hunt-McWilliams Correspondence; Mobile *Register*, August 12, 19, 21, 26, 28, September 4, 19, 1900. For the context of this episode see Kenneth Bailey, *Southern White Protestantism* (New York: Harper & Row, Publishers, 1964), ch. 1.

45. Mary L. Taylor Hunt to Tennant S. McWilliams, June 14, 1972 in Hunt-McWilliams Correspondence; Mobile *Register*, August 12, 26, 28, September 11, 1900.

46. Mobile *Register*, August 22, 24, 28, 29, September 2, 12, 14, 19, 1900. Reelected to Congress in November 1900, George Washington Taylor remained as the First District Representative until 1915. *Biographical Directory of the American Congress*, 1794.

47. Mobile *Register*, September 28, 1900. See Hannis Taylor, *A Treatise on International Public Law* (Chicago: Callahan and Co., 1901).

48. Mobile *Register*, April 14, May 25, 28, June 11–27, 1901; Birmingham *Age-Herald*, April 19, 1901; Birmingham *Ledger*, April 15, 1901; Tuscaloosa *Gazette*, reprinted in Mobile *Register*, April 19, 1901; Hannis Taylor to Thomas M. Owen, April 25, 1901 in Papers of Alabama Historical Society (Manuscripts Division, Alabama State Department of Archives and History, Montgomery, Alabama).

49. Montgomery *Advertiser*, June 4, 1901; Montgomery *Journal*, June 11, 1901; Mobile *Register*, June 12, 27, 1901. Taylor's attitude toward Negro disfranchisement is treated in Chapter V.

50. Mobile *Register*, April 14, 1901; interview with Mary L. Taylor Hunt, December 28, 1971.

Chapter V

1. United States Department of Justice, Spanish Treaty Claims Commission, *Final Report of William Wallace Brown* (Washington, D.C.: Government Printing Office, 1910), 95; St. Louis *Globe Democrat*, March 4, 1902; Mobile *Register*, March 12, 13, 1902. It is clear that Taylor had the credentials to work with the Spanish Treaty Claims Commission owing to his Madrid tenure and his varied legal experience, but the author was unable to determine precisely who helped Taylor obtain the appointment. See Chapter VI for a discussion of Taylor's role before the commission.

2. Mobile *Register*, March 12, 1902.

3. *Mobile City Directory, 1903*, 480.

4. Mobile *Register*, June 4, 1902, December 28, 1922; *Proceedings of the Alabama Bar Association, 1902* (Montgomery: Paragon Press, 1903), 160; *Mobile City Directory, 1902*, 601; *Mobile City Directory, 1903*, 480.

5. Roxana Henson to Tennant S. McWilliams, February 14, 1972 in possession of the author; Hunt, "Memoirs," 18.

6. Mary L. Taylor Hunt to Tennant S. McWilliams, January 21, 1972 in Hunt-McWilliams Correspondence; Hunt, "Memoirs," 14.

7. 58th Cong., 2nd Sess., Senate Document 162, Alaskan Boundary Tribunal, *Proceedings of the Alaskan Boundary Tribunal* (7 vols., Washington: Government Printing Office, 1904), VII, 555–622. Taylor's role before the Alaskan Boundary Tribunal is discussed in Chapter VI.

8. Susan Murray to Tennant S. McWilliams, September 19, 1966 in possession of the author.

9. Hunt, "Memoirs," 19; Roxana Henson to Tennant S. McWilliams, February 14, 1972 in possession of the author; *American Law Review*, XL–XLI (January 1906–December 1907), passim; Roscoe Pound, "Taylor's *Science of Jurisprudence*: A Literary Application of the Doctrine of Accession," *Illinois Law Review*, III (March 1909), 525–33; Henry L. Goody, "Plagiarism—A Fine Art," *Juridicial Review*, XX (January 1909), 302–15; Hannis Taylor to Henry Watterson, March 3, 21, April 19, 1909 in Watterson Papers; Oliver Wendell Holmes to Harold Laski, January 2, 8, December 8, 15, 1917 in Mark DeWolfe Howe, ed., *Holmes-Laski Letters* (2 vols., Cambridge: Harvard University Press, 1941), I, 46–47, 50–51, 118–19.

10. Hannis Taylor to Jacob M. Dickinson and David T. Watson, June 10, 1903, Hannis Taylor to Jacob M. Dickinson, July 6, 1903 in Dickinson Papers; Hannis Taylor to Richard Olney, No. 559, September 14, 1896 in Spain: Despatches.

11. Henry Groves Connor to Hannis Taylor, May 10, June 19, 1917 in Connor Papers; W. H. S. Burgwyn to Walter Clark, September 17, 1906 in *The Papers of Walter Clark*, ed. by Aubrey Lee Brooks and Hugh T. Lefler (2 vols., Chapel Hill: University of North Carolina Press, 1950), II, 82; Hannis Taylor to J. K. Dixon, April 23, 1921 in *Proceedings of the Alabama Bar Association, 1921* (Montgomery: Paragon Press, 1922), 62; Hannis Taylor to T. M. Stevens, July 9, 1914 in *Proceedings of the Alabama Bar Association, 1914* (Montgomery: Paragon Press, 1915), 14; Hannis Taylor to John L. Rapier, August 6, 1904 in possession of Reginia Rapier Marston, Mobile, Alabama; *Cabinet Diaries of Josephus Daniels*, ed. by E. David Cronon (Lincoln: University of Nebraska Press, 1963), 23–24; William Burlie Brown, "The State Literary and History Association, 1900–1950," *North Carolina Historical Review*, XXVIII (April 1951), 159; Mary L. Taylor Hunt to Tennant S. McWilliams, January 21, 1972 in Hunt-McWilliams Correspondence; Palmer Pillans to Tennant S. McWilliams, June 20, 1972 in possession of the author.

12. Richard V. Taylor, "Voice from Alabama," ch. 11, p. 2; interview with Mary L. Taylor Hunt, December 28, 1971. See Taylor, *Origin and Growth of the American Constitution*, 14.

13. Theodore Roosevelt to Hannis Taylor, March 2, November 2, 1905, November 23, December 13, 1916, William Loeb, Jr. to Hannis Taylor, January 22, 1906 in Theodore Roosevelt Papers (Manuscripts Division, Library of Congress, Washington, D.C.).

14. Hunt, "Memoirs," 11–18; Mary L. Taylor Hunt to Tennant S. McWilliams, January 21, 1972 in Hunt-McWilliams Correspondence.

15. Hannis Taylor to Charles Evans Hughes, June 16, 1922 in Applications and Recommendations for Office: Hannis Taylor; Hannis Taylor to Henry Groves Connor, June 18, 1917 in Connor Papers; Jon Reynolds to Tennant S. McWilliams, March 7, 1972 in possession of the author; Walter W. Wright to Tennant S. McWilliams, August 16, 1972 in possession of the author.

16. Interview with Mary L. Taylor Hunt, December 28, 1971.

17. Colman Barry, *The Catholic University of America, 1903-1909: The Rectorship of Dennis J. O'Connel* (Washington: Catholic University of America Press, 1950), 174; Thomas J. Shahan to James Gibbons, May 3, July 6, 1919 in Cardinal James Gibbons Papers (Archives of the Archdiocese of Baltimore, Chancery Building, Baltimore, Maryland); Thomas J. Shahan to Harry M. Daugherty, April 4, 1921 in Applications and Recommendations for Office: Hannis Taylor; Blase Dixon to Tennant S. McWilliams, March 25, April 23, 1972 in possession of the author.

18. Monsignor John F. Donoghue to Tennant S. McWilliams, July 31, 1972 in possession of the author; Mary L. Taylor Hunt to Tennant S. McWilliams, September 8, 1966, April 1, 1969, June 23, 1972 in Hunt-McWilliams Correspondence; Hannis Taylor to Mrs. F. C. Roberts, [n.d.: 1913?] in Roberts Family Papers.

19. The best summary of progressivism—its causes, contradictory forms, and long-term effects—is William L. O'Neill's *The Progressive Years: America Comes of Age* (New York: Dodd, Mead & Co., 1975).

20. George Mowry, *The Era of Theodore Roosevelt* (New York: Harper & Row, Publishers, 1958), passim; John Blum, *The Republican Roosevelt* (Cambridge: Harvard University Press, 1954), passim; Howard K. Beale, *Theodore Roosevelt and the Rise of America to World Power* (Baltimore: Johns Hopkins University Press, 1958), passim; G. Wallace Chessman, *Theodore Roosevelt and the Politics of Power* (Boston: Little Brown & Co.), passim; William H. Harbaugh, *Power and Responsibility: The Life and Times of Theodore Roosevelt* (New York: Farrar, Straus & Giroux, 1961), passim.

21. Mowry, *Era of Theodore Roosevelt*, 144-56; Blum, *Republican Roosevelt*, 37-92; John Blum et al., *The National Experience: A History of the United States* (3rd ed., New York: Harcourt Brace Jovanovich, 1973) 519; Henry May, *The End of American Innocence* (New York: Alfred A. Knopf, 1959), 17, 107.

22. Robert W. Sellen, "Theodore Roosevelt: Historian with a Moral," *Mid-America*, XLI (October 1959), 223-40; John Braeman, *Albert Beveridge* (Chicago: University of Chicago Press, 1971), 316, 323; David Burton, *Theodore Roosevelt: Confident Imperialist* (Philadelphia: University of Pennsylvania Press, 1971), 132-45, 150-57; Richard Hofstadter, *Social Darwinism in Ameri-*

116   NOTES FOR CHAPTER V

can Thought, 1860-1915 (Philadelphia: University of Pennsylvania Press, 1945), 146-73.

23. Taylor, *Origin and Growth of the American Constitution*; Eric F. Goldman, *Rendezvous with Destiny: A History of Modern American Reform* (New York: Random House, 1955), 103-08; Boller, *American Thought in Transition*, 148-74.

24. Hannis Taylor, "Speaker and His Powers," *North American Review*, CLXXXVIII (October 1908), 499-500; Taylor, "Representative Government for Russia," *North American Review*, CLXXX (January 1905), 20-24; Taylor, "Comparative Study of Roman and English Law," *Proceedings of the Louisiana Bar Association, 1898-99* (New Orleans: Grabner Press, 1899), passim.; Taylor, "Due Process of Law," *Yale Law Journal*, XXIV (March 1915), 353-69; Taylor, "A Government of Law As Distinguished from a Government of Functionaries," *The Green Bag*, XVIII (June 1906), 489-95; Taylor, "Genesis of the Supreme Court," *Case and Comment*, XVIII (June 1911), 3-7; Taylor, "What We Owe to the Magna Charta," *New York Times*, June 13, 1915; Taylor, "A New Era in Legal Government," *North American Review*, CLXXXIX (May 1909), 640-43; Taylor, "Constitutional Nationalism," *American Law Review*, XLI (November 1907), 892-93; Taylor, "A Bancroftian Invention," *Yale Law Journal*, XVIII (December 1908), 75-84; Taylor, *Origin and Growth of the American Constitution*, 1-137; Taylor, *Jurisdiction and Procedure of the Supreme Court*, 1-36.

25. Taylor's view of the Confederation and Constitution periods reflects an acceptance of John Fiske's "critical period" thesis. Taylor, "Genesis of the Supreme Court," 1-7; Taylor, "Five Master-Builders of the American Commonwealth," *Second Safe and Sane Celebration of Independence Day at the National Capital* (Washington: Superintendent of Documents, 1910), 4-7; Taylor, "Legitimate Functions of Judge-Made Law," *The Green Bag*, XVII (October 1905), 557-65; Taylor, *Origin and Growth of the American Constitution*, 139-220. Taylor doggedly advanced the notion that Pelatiah Webster, a Philadelphia attorney, formulated many rudiments of the federal system which the official delegates to the convention later developed. See Taylor, "The 125th Anniversary of the Drafting of the Constitution of the United States," *Georgetown Law Journal*, I (November 1912), 1-16; Taylor, "The Designer of the Constitution of the United States," *North American Review*, CLXXXV (August 1907), 813-24; Taylor, "Pelatiah Webster: Architect of Our Federal Constitution," *Yale Law Journal*, XVII (December 1907), 73-85; Taylor, "Pelatiah Webster's Plan of the Constitution," *Congressional Record*, 60th Cong., 1st Sess. (1908), 5630-38; Taylor, "Petition Presented to Congress . . . on the Anniversary of the Pelatiah Webster's Tract," *Congressional Record*,

63rd Cong., 2nd Sess. (1914), 3588–91. For samples of the rejection of the Webster thesis see Robert Livingston Shuyler, *The Constitution of the United States* (New York: Macmillan Co., 1923), 159–60; Gaillard Hunt, *Pelatiah Webster and the Constitution* (Washington: Government Printing Office, 1912), passim.; Max Farrand, *The Framing of the Constitution of the United States* (New Haven: Yale University Press, 1913), 53.

26. Taylor, *Origin and Growth of the American Constitution*, 253, 295.

27. Taylor, "Five Master-Builders," 8; Taylor, "The American Commonwealth," in *Congressional Record*, 62nd Cong., 2nd Sess. (1912), 335; Taylor, "Constitutional Nationalism," 553–54; Taylor, "Elasticity of Written Constitutions," *North American Review*, CLXXXII (February 1906), 210–14.

28. Taylor, *Due Process of Law and Equal Protection of the Law* (Chicago: Callahan and Co., 1917), 134–452; Taylor, *Origin and Growth of the American Constitution*, 401–04, 412; Taylor, *The Science of Jurisprudence* (New York: Macmillan Co., 1908), 582; Taylor, "The Impending Conflict," *North American Review*, CLXXXIII (July 1906), 30.

29. Taylor, "Startling Growth of State Power," *North American Review*, CXC (October 1909), 462; Taylor, "Growing Importance of the Fourteenth Amendment," *American Law Review*, XLI (July 1907), 559–60; Taylor, "American Commonwealth," 335; Taylor, "Legitimate Functions of Judge-Made Law," 565; Taylor, *Origin and Growth of the American Constitution*, 404–10. Roosevelt's philosophy of corporate regulation is analyzed in Blum, *Roosevelt*, 73–105 and in Richard Hofstadter, "Theodore Roosevelt: The Conservative as Progressive," *The American Political Tradition and the Men Who Made It* (New York: Random House, 1948), 222. On the Supreme Court's support of vested rights see Arnold M. Paul, *Conservative Crisis and the Rule of Law: Attitudes of Bar and Bench, 1887–1895* (Ithaca, N.Y.: Cornell University Press, 1960), passim.

30. Taylor, *Origin and Growth of the American Constitution*, 298, 435–39, 441–42; Taylor, *Due Process*, 760ff. See Gabriel Kolko, *Triumph of Conservatism: A Re-interpretation of American History, 1900–1916* (New York: Free Press of Glencoe, 1963), 125–27 for comments on this early controversy involving the American Tobacco Company.

31. Taylor, "Startling Growth of State Power," 462–63; Taylor, "Impending Conflict," 26, 32; Taylor, *Due Process*, 340, 487, 611–48. Other progressives, especially Roosevelt, often expressed similar fears of socialism. See for instance Theodore Roosevelt to C. F. Gettemy, February 1, 1905 in *The Letters of Theodore Roosevelt*, ed. by E. E. Morison (8 vols., Cambridge: Harvard University Press, 1951–1954), IV, 113.

32. Taylor, "Growing Importance of the Fourteenth Amendment," 558; Taylor, *Origin and Growth of the American Constitution*, 407, 413; Taylor, *Due Process*, 421, 760–819.

33. *Fred J. Bliss v. Washoe Copper and Anaconda Copper Company*, 223 *United States Reports* 733–34 (1913).

34. *Hitchman Coal and Coke Company v. John Mitchell, et al.*, 245 *United States Reports*, 229–74 (1916); *James B. Roberts, Administrator of the Estate of Argus McNeil, deceased v. Tennessee Coal, Iron and Railway Company*, 250 *United States Reports* 659 (1919); Hannis Taylor to Simeon E. Baldwin, December 21, 1916 and Willis Van Devanter to Hannis Taylor, [n.d.] in Baldwin Family Papers (Manuscripts Division, Yale University Library, New Haven, Connecticut); Hannis Taylor to Henry St. George Tucker, September 11, 1914 in Tucker Papers.

35. Taylor, *Origin and Growth of the American Constitution*, 422–23; Taylor, *Due Process*, 411, 662–63; Taylor, "Due Process," 361.

36. Taylor, "Impending Conflict," 30–31; Taylor, "Independence of the Federal Judiciary," *American Law Review*, XL (July–August, 1906), 490–95; Taylor, "Elasticity of Written Constitutions," 214. For discussions of the Hepburn bill, see Gabriel Kolko, *Railroads and Regulation, 1877–1916* (Princeton: Princeton University Press, 1965), 140–44; Blum, *Roosevelt*, 87–105.

37. Loren P. Beth, *The Development of the American Constitution, 1877–1917* (New York: Harper & Row, Publishers, 1971), passim.; Paul L. Murphy, *The Constitution in Crisis Times, 1918–1969* (New York: Harper & Row, Publishers, 1972), 1–169.

38. Hannis Taylor to Thomas Goode Jones, April 14, 27, May 1, 1907 in Thomas Goode Jones Papers; Taylor, "Due Process," 363. Five years before he died Taylor published a full study on this subject, *Due Process of Law and Equal Protection of the Law*, passim. Also see Taylor, "Due Process of Law: Persistent and Harmful Influence of *Murray v. Hoboken Land and Improvement Company*," *Yale Law Journal*, XXIV (March 1915), 353–69.

39. *Mobile, Jackson, and Kansas City Railroad Company, et al. v. State of Mississippi, et al.*, 210 *United States Reports* 187–206 (1908). The author also consulted briefs for this case, which are in the Supreme Court Library, Washington, D.C. Taylor's railroad cases include *Texas and Pacific Railroad Company v. Abilene Cotton Oil Company*, 204 *United States Reports* 426–48 (1907); *Railroad Commission of the State of Mississippi, et al. v. Louisville and Nashville Railroad Company*, 225 *United States Reports*, 272–81 (1912); *Alabama and Vicksburg Railway Company, et al. v. The Railroad Commission of the State of Mississippi*, 203 *United States Reports* 496–501 (1906); *Yazoo and Mississippi Valley Railroad Company v. Mayor and Alderman of Vicksburg*, 209 *United States Reports* 358–65 (1908).

40. Hannis Taylor, "Minnesota Rate Cases," *Harvard Law Review*, XVII (November 1913), 14–26.

41. Hannis Taylor to John Tyler Morgan, February 23, 1887 in Morgan Papers; Taylor, "The House of Representatives and the House of Commons," *North American Review*, CLIX (August 1894), 225–34; Taylor, "Outlook for Parliamentary Government," *North American Reivew*, CLX (April 1895), 479–91; Taylor, "Powers of the French President," *North American Review*, CLXIV (February 1897), 129–38; Taylor, "Inefficiency of Congress as a Legislative Body," *Proceedings of the Alabama Bar, 1886* (Montgomery: Barrett Printers, 1887), 88–101; Taylor, "National House of Representatives," *Atlantic Monthly*, LXV (June 1890), 766–73.

42. Oscar Kraines, "The President Versus the Congress: the Keep Commission, 1905–1909, the First Comprehensive Presidential Inquiry into Administration," *Western Political Science Quarterly*, XXIII (March 1970), 5–54.

43. Taylor, "Speaker and His Powers," 495–503. Since Taylor explicitly directed his comments at the office of Speaker instead of at any given personality, it is doubtful that he intended the article as part of the developing progressive revolt against Speaker Joseph Cannon, which climaxed in 1910. See Kelley and Harbison, *American Constitution*, 626–29.

44. Blum, *Roosevelt*, 73–123; Kelley and Harbison, *American Constitution*, 587–89.

45. Hannis Taylor, "An Interstate Code Commission," *Proceedings of the Alabama Bar, 1881* (Montgomery: Barrett Printers, 1882) 210–33.

46. Hannis Taylor, "Unification of American Law," *The Green Bag*, XXII (May 1910), 269. For views of other attorneys and the business leaders they often represented see, for example, Edward A. Gilmore, "Legislative Cooperation Among the States," *American Bar Association Journal*, VII (February 1921), 74; Charles P. Sherman, "One Code for All States," *The Green Bag*, XXV (November 1913), 460–67; Robert H. Wiebe, *The Search for Order, 1877–1920* (New York: Hill & Wang, 1967), 177; James Weinstein, *The Corporate Ideal in the Liberal State, 1900–1918* (Boston: Beacon Press, 1968) 31–32.

47. Taylor, "Unification of American Law," 267–74; Taylor, "Minnesota Rate Cases," 25–26; Taylor, *Origin and Growth of the American Constitution*, 471–73. Also see I. L. Sharfman *The Interstate Commerce Commission: A Study in Administrative Law and Procedure* (4 vols., New York: The Commonwealth Fund, 1931), II, 233; Weinstein, *Corporate Ideal in the Liberal State*, 29–30.

48. Woodward, *Origins of the New South*, 369–428.

49. See Chapter II.

50. Taylor, "Alabama," *Encyclopaedia Britannica*, 238–39; Taylor, Speech to Confederate Veterans printed in Montgomery *Advertiser*, June 4, 1901;

Malcolm C. McMillan, *Constitutional Development in Alabama, 1798–1901: A Study in Politics, the Negro, and Sectionalism* (Chapel Hill: University of North Carolina Press, 1955), 240–60; David Alan Harris, "Racists and Reformers: A Study of Progressivism in Alabama, 1896–1911" (Ph.D. dissertation, University of North Carolina, 1967), passim.

51. Jack Temple Kirby, *Darkness at the Dawning: Race and Reform in the Progressive Era* (Philadelphia: J. B. Lippincott Co., 1972), passim.; Dewey Grantham, "The Progressive Movement and the Negro," *South Atlantic Quarterly*, LIV (October 1955), 461–77; Seth M. Scheiner, "President Theodore Roosevelt and the Negro, 1901–1908," *Journal of Negro History*, XLVII (July 1962), 169–82; and especially Thomas G. Dyer, "Theodore Roosevelt and the Idea of Race" (Ph.D. dissertation, University of Georgia, 1975), passim.

52. Mary L. Taylor Hunt to Tennant S. McWilliams, January 21, 1972 in Hunt-McWilliams Correspondence; Taylor, "Five Master-Builders," 8; Taylor, "American Commonwealth," 334; Taylor, *Origin and Growth of the American Constitution*, 374–75.

53. Taylor, *Origin and Growth of the American Constitution*, 376; Taylor, "The Solid South: A National Calamity," *North American Review*, CLXXXIX (January 1909), 3–4; August Meier, *Negro Thought in America, 1880–1915: Racial Ideologies in the Age of Booker T. Washington* (Ann Arbor: University of Michigan Press, 1963), passim.

54. Arthur F. Raper, *The Tragedy of Lynching* (Chapel Hill: University of North Carolina Press, 1933), 480–83; Taylor, "True Remedy for Lynch Law," *American Law Review*, XLI (March 1907), 255–64.

55. Taylor, "True Remedy for Lynch Law," 264–66.

56. Vincent P. DeSantis, *Republicans Face the Southern Question: The New Departure Years, 1877–1897* (Baltimore: Johns Hopkins University Press, 1959), passim.; Stanley P. Hirshon, *Farewell to the Bloody Shirt: Northern Republicans and the Southern Negro* (Bloomington: Indiana University Press, 1962), passim.; Woodward, *Origins of the New South*, 462–69.

57. E. Merton Coulter, "The Attempt of William Howard Taft to Break the Solid South," *Georgia Historical Quarterly*, XIX (June 1935), 134–44; Woodward, *Origins of the New South*, 462–69.

58. Theodore Roosevelt to Hannis Taylor, November 2, 1905, January 2, 1909 in Roosevelt Papers; William Howard Taft to Hannis Taylor, March 13, 1909 in Taft Papers; Hannis Taylor to Henry Watterson, March 21, 1909 in Watterson Papers; Woodward, *Origins of the New South*, 465–66.

59. Taylor, "Solid South: A National Calamity," 1–10.

60. James W. Garner, "Southern Politics Since the Civil War," in *Studies in Southern History and Politics Inscribed to William Archibald Dunning* (New York:

Columbia University Press, 1914), 383–84; Coulter, "William Howard Taft's Attempt to Break the Solid South," 142. George Brown Tindall interprets recent Southern politics in *The Disruption of the Solid South* (Athens: University of Georgia Press, 1972).

61. The contradictions of progressivism are explored in David Noble, *The Progressive Mind, 1890–1917* (Chicago: Rand McNally & Co., 1971), 152–64; Noble, *The Paradox of Progressive Thought* (Minneapolis: University of Minnesota Press, 1958), passim.

62. Theodore Roosevelt to Hannis Taylor, October 28, 1908 in Roosevelt Papers.

Chapter VI

1. *Messages and Papers of Presidents*, XIV, 6718.

2. John Milton Cooper, Jr., "Progressivism and American Foreign Policy: A Reconsideration," *Mid-America*, LI (October 1969), 264–69. See also William E. Leuchtenburg, "Progressivism and Imperialism: The Progressive Movement and American Foreign Policy," *Mississippi Valley Historical Review*, XXXIX (December 1952), 483–504; Monroe P. Billington, "Senator Thomas P. Gore: Southern Isolationist," *Southwestern Social Science Quarterly*, XLII (March 1962), 381–89.

3. Cooper, "Progressivism and American Foreign Policy," 261–64; Beale, *Theodore Roosevelt and the Rise of America to World Power*, 23–28. Few historians deny that Roosevelt was an imperialist; difference of opinion develops, rather, on the question of Roosevelt's motivation. Studies showing Roosevelt as one determined to rule other people as an exercise in personal ego and nationalism include Hofstadter, "Theodore Roosevelt: The Conservative as Progressive," 212–15; Henry F. Pringle, *Theodore Roosevelt* (New York: Harcourt, Brace & World, 1931), 166–67; Robert Endicott Osgood, *Ideals and Self-Interest in American Foreign Relations: The Great Transformation of the Twentieth Century* (Chicago: University of Chicago Press, 1958), 43–47, 88–91, 135–53; Burton, *Theodore Roosevelt: Confident Imperialist*, passim.; William A. Williams, *The Tragedy of American Diplomacy* (New York: Delta Publishing Co., 1962), 53–61; Lloyd C. Gardner, "American Foreign Policy, 1900–1921," in *Towards A New Past: Dissenting Essays in American History*, ed. by Barton Bernstein (New York: Random House, 1967), 208–11. Roosevelt's less negative characteristics—his desire for order and efficiency in world affairs, his talents as an administrator—are emphasized in Beale, *Theodore Roosevelt and the Rise of America to World Power*, passim.; Chessman, *Theodore Roosevelt and the Politics of Power*, 94–128; Harbaugh, *Power and Responsibility*,

270ff; Blum, *Republican Roosevelt*, 61–63, 151–59, ch. 8; Mowry, *Era of Theodore Roosevelt*, 143–64, 181–96, 274–86.

4. St. Louis *Globe-Democrat*, March 14, 1902; Mobile *Register*, March 12, 13, June 7, 1902; Mary L. Taylor Hunt to Tennant S. McWilliams, April 1, 1969 in Hunt-McWilliams Correspondence.

5. United States Department of Justice, Spanish Treaty Claims Commission, *Final Report of William Wallace Brown* (Washington: Government Printing Office, 1910), passim.; Department of Justice, Spanish Treaty Claims Commission, *Final Report of William E. Fuller* (Washington: Government Printing Office, 1907), passim.; John Bassett Moore, *Collected Papers* (New Haven: Yale University Press, 1945), 301–02; United States National Archives, *National Archives Guide*, (Washington: Government Printing Office, 1940), 96.

6. Hannis Taylor, "The Spanish Treaty Claims Commission," *North American Review*, CLXXXII (May 1906), 738–46.

7. Richard V. Taylor, "Voice from Alabama," ch. 11, p. 2.

8. William E. Chandler to William A. Maury, August 26, 1902 in Spain: Claims, 1901, Miscellaneous Correspondence of William E. Chandler (Civil Archives Branch, National Archives, Washington, D.C.); Notes of Meetings of the Spanish Treaty Claims Commission made by William E. Chandler, 1901–1907 (Civil Archives Branch, National Archives, Washington, D.C.); Leonard Burr Richardson, *William E. Chandler, Republican* (New York: Dodd, Mead & Co., 1940), 642, 644, 728.

9. Charles Souter Campbell, *Anglo-American Understanding, 1898–1903* (Baltimore: Johns Hopkins University Press, 1957), 301–05; Charles Callahan Tansill, *Canadian-American Relations, 1895–1911* (New Haven: Yale University Press, 1943), chs. 5–8; William M. Malloy, comp., *Treaties, Conventions, International Acts, Protocols and Agreements, 1776–1909* (2 vols., Washington: Government Printing Office, 1910), I, 787–92.

10. Thomas A. Bailey, "Theodore Roosevelt and the Alaskan Boundary Settlement," *Canadian Historical Review*, XVIII (June 1937), 123–30; Charles G. Washburn, "Memoir of Henry Cabot Lodge," *Massachusetts Historical Society Proceedings*, LVIII (1925), 339–41; William Rascoe Thayer, *The Life and Letters of John Hay* (2 vols., Boston: Houghton Mifflin Co., 1908), II, 211; John W. Foster, "The Alaskan Boundary Tribunal," *National Geographic Magazine*, XV (December 1904), 10; John W. Foster, *Diplomatic Memoirs* (2 vols., Boston: Houghton Mifflin Co., 1909), II, 201; Royal Cortissoz, *Life and Letters of Whitelaw Reid* (2 vols., New York: Charles Scribner's Sons, 1921), II, 268; Hannis Taylor to Jacob M. Dickinson, July 6, 1903 in Dickinson Papers; Hilary Herbert to John Hay, March 30, 1903 in Applications and Recommendations for Office: Hannis Taylor.

11. For the complete text of Taylor's argument see 58th Cong., 2nd Sess., Senate Document 162, Alaskan Boundary Tribunal, *Proceedings of the Alaskan Boundary Tribunal* (7 vols., Washington: Government Printing Office, 1904), VII, 555–622. Also see London *Times*, September 30, October 1, 1903.

12. *Proceedings of the Alaskan Boundary Tribunal*, VII, 561–62.

13. Ibid., 611–12.

14. Ibid., 618.

15. London *Times*, October 16, 20, 1903; Mobile *Register*, October 20, 1903.

16. Henry Cabot Lodge to Theodore Roosevelt, September 29, 1903 in *Correspondence of Henry Cabot Lodge and Theodore Roosevelt*, II, 61; Theodore Roosevelt to Hannis Taylor, March 15, 1904, February 20, 1911 in Roosevelt Papers; Washburn, "Memoir of Henry Cabot Lodge," 341. For the text of the Alaskan Boundary Tribunal award see *Proceedings of the Alaskan Boundary Tribunal*, I, Part 1, 31–32.

17. On Roosevelt's views see, for example, Burton, *Theodore Roosevelt: Confident Imperialist*, 145–47.

18. Taylor, "Work of the Peace Commission," 744–45; Taylor, "Is Colonization a Crime?," 739–41; Taylor, *Origin and Growth of the American Constitution*, ch. 12; Taylor, "Conquered Territory and the Constitution," 580–86; Taylor, "Lord Haldane and the Monroe Doctrine," *Georgetown Law Journal*, II (June 1914), 1–5; Taylor, "Origin and Growth of the Law of Neutrality," *Georgetown Law Journal*, III (March 1915), 6; Taylor, "International Conference at Rio de Janeiro," *American Law Review*, XL (November–December 1906), 899.

19. Taylor, "International Arbitration: The Product of the Modern International System," *The Green Bag*, XVII (February 1905), 104.

20. Burton, *Theodore Roosevelt: Confident Imperialist*, 101–20; Harbaugh, *Power and Responsibility*, 191–97, 234–36; Beale, *Theodore Roosevelt and the Rise of America to World Power*, 29.

21. Taylor, "International Conference at Rio de Janeiro," 906–07.

22. Ibid., 905–07; Taylor, "International Arbitration," 102–03; Taylor, "International Arbitration and the Pan American Conference," *North American Review*, CLXXIV (March 1902), 303–14; Theodore Roosevelt to Augustus O. Bacon, April 11, 1906 in Roosevelt Papers; Hannis Taylor to Elihu Root, April 24, 1906, and Hannis Taylor to John Sharpe Williams, April 7, 1906 in Applications and Recommendations for Office: Hannis Taylor.

23. Dwight Carroll Miner, *The Fight for the Panama Route* (New York: Columbia University Press, 1940), 200–397; Burton, *Theodore Roosevelt: Confident Imperialist*, 120–30.

24. Hannis Taylor to Theodore Roosevelt, July 24, 1912 in Roosevelt

Papers; Taylor, *Origin and Growth of the American Constitution*, 396; Taylor, "Is Colonization a Crime?," 744.

25. Burton, *Theodore Roosevelt: Confident Imperailist*, 83.

26. Taylor, "Conquered Territory and the Constitution," 586–89.

27. Oscar M. Alonso, *Theodore Roosevelt and the Philippines, 1897–1907* (Quezon City: University of the Philippines Press, 1970), passim.; Burton, *Theodore Roosevelt: Confident Imperialist*, 83.

28. Taylor, "Is Colonization a Crime?," 737–38, 743–44; Taylor, "American Commonwealth," 334. See *Dorr v. United States*, 195 *United States Reports* 138–39 (1904).

29. Henry Cabot Lodge to Theodore Roosevelt, February 21, 1911 and Hannis Taylor to Theodore Roosevelt, February 21, 1911 in Roosevelt Papers.

30. Beale, *Theodore Roosevelt and the Rise of America to World Power*, chs. 4, 5, and 6.

31. Ibid., 67, 333–52; Harbaugh, *Power and Responsibility*, 293–94.

32. Taylor, *Treatise on International Public Law*, v.

33. Taylor, "International Arbitration and the Pan American Conference," 307, 311; Taylor, "Growth of Hague Ideals," *American Law Review*, XL (January–February 1906), 1–8; Taylor, "National Maritime Rights and Responsibilities in Time of War," *North American Review*, CLXXXI (August 1905), 161–62; Taylor, "International Arbitration," 102–04; Taylor, "International Conference at Rio de Janeiro," 906; Taylor, "The Papacy As an International Power," *American Law Review*, XLI (September 1907), 728; Taylor, *Science of Jurisprudence*, 610.

34. Roosevelt's Japanese policy is well covered in Raymond A. Esthus, *Theodore Roosevelt and Japan* (Seattle: University of Washington Press, 1966), 56–96. For his role in the Algeciras Conference that settled Moroccan disturbances see Harbaugh, *Power and Responsibility*, 290, and Beale, *Theodore Roosevelt and the Rise of America to World Power*, 372–85. The ill-fated arbitration treaties are discussed in W. Stull Holt, *Treaties Defeated by the Senate* (Baltimore: Johns Hopkins University Press, 1933), 204–12, and in John P. Campbell, "Taft, Roosevelt, and the Arbitration Treaties of 1911," *Journal of American History*, LIII (September 1966), 279–98.

35. Taylor, "National Maritime Rights," 161–68; Taylor, "Neutral Territorial Waters As a Naval Base," *American Law Review*, XL (May–June 1906), 407–08; Taylor, "The Growing Conception of Neutrality," *American Law Review*, XL (March–April 1906), 257–59; Taylor, *Origin and Growth of the American Constitution*, 399–401; Taylor, "Spheres of Influence and Protectorates," *American Law Review*, XLI (January 1907), 98; Taylor, "Congo: A Free State," *American Law Review*, XLI (January 1907), 106–07.

36. Taylor, "International Arbitration," 104; Taylor, "American Commonwealth," 334–35; Lawrence S. Abbott to Theodore Roosevelt, February 8, 1905 in Roosevelt Papers; Oliver, "Centennial Celebration," 6–7.

37. Arthur S. Link, *Woodrow Wilson and the Progressive Era, 1910–1917* (New York: Harper & Row, Publishers, 1954), 3–6, 13–16, 22–24; Taylor, *A Review of President Wilson's Administration* (Washington: [n.p.], 1916), 1; interview with Mary L. Taylor Hunt, December 28, 1971.

38. Taylor, "Solid South: A National Calamity," 1–10; Taylor, *Review of President Wilson's Administration*, 1.

39. For the role of the Southern expatriate in Wilson's election, see Woodward, *Origins of the New South*, 471ff.

40. Taylor, *Review of President Wilson's Administration*, 1; interview with Mary L. Taylor Hunt, December 28, 1971.

41. Hannis Taylor to Woodrow Wilson, January 7, 1913 in Wilson Papers.

42. P. B. McCarthy to Woodrow Wilson, March 6, 11, 1914 in Applications and Recommendations for Office: Hannis Taylor.

43. Edward S. Corwin to Woodrow Wilson, March 8, 1914 in Applications and Recommendations for Office: Hannis Taylor; interview with Mary L. Taylor Hunt, December 28, 1971.

44. E. Taylor Parks, *Colombia and the United States, 1765–1934* (Durham: Duke University Press, 1935), 440–41.

45. Hannis Taylor, *Why the Pending Treaty With Colombia Should Be Ratified* (Washington: [n.p.], 1914), passim. See reprint in *Congressional Record*, 63rd Cong., 2nd Sess. (1914), 12369–72.

46. *Washington Post*, June 18–22, 1914; *New York Times*, June 18–19, 1914; Mary L. Taylor Hunt to Tennant S. McWilliams, August 17, 1966, December 18, 1968, January 21, 1972 in Hunt-McWilliams Correspondence; Hunt, "Memoirs," 10.

47. Interview with Mary L. Taylor Hunt, December 28, 1971.

48. Arthur S. Link, *Wilson: The New Freedom* (Princeton: Princeton University Press, 1956), 304–14; William S. Coker, "The Panama Canal Tolls Controversy," *Journal of American History*, LV (December 1965), 555–64.

49. Theodore Roosevelt to Arthur Lee Hamilton, August 14, 1912 in *Letters of Theodore Roosevelt*, VII, 596–98.

50. Hannis Taylor, "The Two Great Canals," *National Waterways: A Magazine of Transportation*, I (November 1912), 105–10.

51. *New York Times*, April 17, 1913; Hannis Taylor, "The Panama Canal: The Rule of Treaty Construction Known as *Rebus Sic Stantibus*," *Georgetown Law Journal*, I (May 1913), 193–201. At the request of Mississippi Senator James K. Vardaman, a Democrat who opposed Wilson's revised tolls policy,

excerpts from Taylor's articles were reprinted in *Congressional Record*, 63rd Cong., 1st Sess. (1913), 1511. Also see Holmes, *White Chief*, 294–97.

52. Link, *Woodrow Wilson and the Progressive Era*, 107–44.

53. Taylor, *Review of President Wilson's Administration*, 2–23.

54. Blum, *Republican Roosevelt*, 151; Harbaugh, *Power and Responsibility*, 479.

55. Taylor, *Review of President Wilson's Administration*, 21–23.

56. Link, *Woodrow Wilson and the Progressive Era*, 145–73.

57. On Roosevelt see Blum, *Republican Roosevelt*, 151–53; Harbaugh, *Power and Responsibility*, 467–75.

58. Taylor, "Our Rights and Duties As a Neutral Nation," *Proceedings of the Alabama Bar Association, 1915* (Montgomery: Paragon Press, 1915), 130–42. See also Taylor, "Origin and Growth of the Law of Neutrality." 1; *New York Times*, February 7, 8, August 1, 1915, May 18, 1917, December 10, 1918.

59. Taylor, "Our Rights and Duties as a Neutral Nation," 142; Arthur S. Link, "The Cotton Crisis, the South and Anglo-American Diplomacy, 1914–1915," *Studies in Southern History in Memory of Albert Ray Newsome, 1894–1951* (Chapel Hill: University of North Carolina Press, 1957), 122–38.

60. George Brown Tindall, *The Emergence of the New South 1913–1945* (Baton Rouge: Louisiana State University Press, 1967), 36–46; Link, *Woodrow Wilson and the Progressive Era*, 174–97.

61. Taylor, *Review of President Wilson's Administration*, 1–17, 26–28.

62. Ibid., 19–20. See Hannis Taylor, *Shall We Perpetuate the Wilson Dictatorship As a System of Government?* (Washington: [n.p.], 1916), passim.; *New York Times*, December 23, 1916; New York *Herald*, March 28, 1919; Hannis Taylor to Theodore Roosevelt, November 23, 1916, and Theodore Roosevelt to Hannis Taylor, November 28, 1916 in Roosevelt Papers; Paul L. Murphy, *The Meaning of Freedom of Speech: First Amendment Freedoms from Wilson to FDR* (Westport, Conn.: Greenwood Press, 1972), 297.

63. Link, *Woodrow Wilson and the Progressive Era*, 252–82; Murphy, *Constitution in Crisis Times*, 12–13. Although Roosevelt became enthusiastic about a volunteer army, he nevertheless supported most of Wilson's conscription act, including the provision on militia. See Joe Frank Decker, "Progressive Reaction to Selective Service in World War I" (Ph.D dissertation, University of Georgia, 1969), 67–88.

64. Tindall, *Emergence of the New South*, 41–42; Alex Matthews Arnett, *Claude Kitchin and the Wilson War Policies* (Boston: Houghton Mifflin Co., 1939), passim.; Holmes, *White Chief*, 294–327.

65. Belle Case LaFollette and Fola LaFollette, *Robert M. LaFollette* (2 vols., New York: Macmillan Co., 1953), II, 738; Hannis Taylor, "An Appeal to

Congress to Prevent the Sending of Conscripted National Militia to European Battle Fields," *Congressional Record*, 65th Cong., 1st Sess. (1917), Appendix, 640–43; Taylor, "Is the Draft Law Constitutional?," *Lafollette's Magazine*, IX (June 1917), 4–5; Taylor, "National Militia Cannot Be Sent Abroad," *Congressional Record*, 65th Cong., 3rd Sess. (1917), 6633; Taylor, *Loyalty to the Constitution* (Washington: [n.p.], 1917), passim.

66. *Cox v. Wood*, 247 *United States Reports* 3–7 (1918).

67. Case file on *Cox v. Wood* (Civil Archives Division, National Archives, Washington, D.C.); *United States Supreme Court Docket, October Term, 1917* (Washington: National Archives, 1954), Microcopy 216, roll 15.

68. *Selective Draft Law Cases*, 245 *United States Reports*, 366–90 (1918).

69. Appellant's brief in case file on *Cox v. Wood*.

70. Ibid.

71. Appellee's brief in case file on *Cox v. Wood*.

72. Oliver Wendell Holmes to Harold Laski, January 2, 8, December 26, 28, 1916, December 8, 15, 1917 in Mark DeWolfe Howe, ed., *Holmes-Laske Letters*, I, 46–47, 50–51, 118–19; Oliver Wendell Holmes to Sir Frederick Pollack, June 14, 18, 1918, April 27, 1919 in Mark DeWolfe Howe, ed., *Holmes-Pollack Letters* (2 vols., Cambridge: Harvard University Press, 1941), I, 143–44, 267, II, 11; E. David Cronon, ed., *The Cabinet Diaries of Josephus Daniels 1913–1921* (Lincoln: University of Nebraska Press, 1963), 165; Taylor, "Reminiscences [of Hannis Taylor]," 16–17; Paul L. Murphy to Tennant S. McWilliams, December 5, 1972 in possession of the author.

73. See the full text of the Court's decision in case file on *Cox v. Wood*. Also see *Cox v. Wood*, 247 *United States Reports* 3–7 (1918); *New York Times*, December 10, 1918; Edward S. Corwin, *Total War and the Constitution* (New York: Alfred A. Knopf, 1947), 87–88; Murphy, *Constitution in Crisis in Times*, 13; Carl Brent Swisher, *American Constitutional Development* (Boston: Houghton Mifflin Co., 1954), 602.

74. Mary L. Taylor Hunt to Tennant S. McWilliams, August 17, 1966, December 18, 1968 in Hunt-McWilliams Correspondence; Hunt, "Memoirs," 8, 19.

75. For Roosevelt's views see Harbaugh, *Power and Responsibility*, 516–19; Burton, *Theodore Roosevelt: Confident Imperialist*, 196–98.

76. Thomas A. Bailey, *Woodrow Wilson and the Lost Peace* (New York: MacMillan Co., 1944), 21ff.

77. *New York Times*, January 24, 1917.

78. *Congressional Record*, 65th Cong., 3rd Sess. (1919), 27–28; see also Taylor's "The People Must Decide," submitted to the Senate by James K. Vardaman, in ibid., 3656–58.

79. Harbaugh, *Power and Responsibility*, 516; Burton, *Theodore Roosevelt: Confident Imperialist*, 197.

80. New York *Herald*, March 28, April 21, 1919.

81. Hannis Taylor, "The Pending Appeal to the American People to Sign Their Own Death Warrant," *Congressional Record*, 66th Cong., 1st Sess. (1919), 4722–25; Taylor, *Let Us Return to the Faith of Our Fathers* (Washington: [n.p.], 1919), 4–5, 12–15; O. E. Welles to Harry M. Daugherty, March 10, 1921 in Applications and Recommendations for Office: Hannis Taylor; interview with Mary L. Taylor Hunt, December 28, 1971.

82. Interview with Mary L. Taylor Hunt, December 28, 1971.

83. P. J. McCumber to Harry M. Daugherty, May 10, 1921, Henry S. New to Harry M. Daugherty, January 16, 1922, Miles V. Poindexter to Harry M. Daugherty, March 8, 1921 in Applications and Recommendations for Office: Hannis Taylor; Taylor, *Let Us Return to the Faith of Our Fathers*, 14–15; Robert K. Murray, *The Harding Era* (Minneapolis: University of Minnesota Press, 1969), 106–08.

84. Hannis Taylor to Mary L. Taylor Hunt, April 14, 1922 in Hunt-McWilliams Correspondence; Charles Evans Hughes to Hannis Taylor, July 22, 1922, Hannis Taylor to Charles Evans Hughes, June 16, 1922 in Applications and Recommendations for Office: Hannis Taylor.

85. Taylor, "Triumph of American Diplomacy," *National Republican*, April 22, 29, 1922, reprinted in *Congressional Record*, 67th Cong., 2nd Sess. (1922), 7888–95. See also L. Ethan Ellis, *Republican Foreign Policy, 1921–23* (New Brunswick: Rutgers University Press, 1968), 79–139; J. Chal Vinson, *William E. Borah and the Outlawry of War* (Athens: University of Georgia Press, 1957), 31–47.

86. Interview with Mary L. Taylor Hunt, December 28, 1971.

87. Ibid.; Mary L. Taylor Hunt to Tennant S. McWilliams, August 17, December 18, 1966, January 21, 1972 in Hunt-McWilliams Correspondence; Parks, *Colombia and the United States*, 441–57; Harbaugh, *Power and Responsibility*, 465.

88. Williams, *Tragedy of American Diplomacy*, 84ff; Burton, *Theodore Roosevelt: Confident Imperialist*, vii.

89. Washington *Evening Star*, December 27, 1922; interview with Mary L. Taylor Hunt, December 28, 1971.

90. Mobile *Register*, December 28, 1922; Washington *Evening Star*, December 27, 1922; *New York Times*, December 27, 1922; Hunt, "Memoirs," 4; Mary L. Taylor Hunt to Tennant S. McWilliams, December 18, 1968 in Hunt-McWilliams Correspondence.

91. St. Matthew's Church Register of Deaths (Rectory, St. Matthew's Church, Washington, D.C.); Monsignor John K. Kuhn to Tennant S.

McWilliams, May 16, 1972 in possession of the author; *Washington Post*, December 29, 1922; Hunt, "Memoirs," 3.

Epilogue

1. C. Vann Woodward, *The Burden of Southern History* (Rev. ed., Baton Rouge: Louisiana State University Press, 1970), 3–26, 187–234.

2. For other comments on the significance of the Southerner in the American experience, see Charles Grier Sellers, Jr., ed., *The Southerner as American* (Chapel Hill: University of North Carolina Press, 1960), passim.; Sheldon Hackney, "Origins of the New South in Retrospect," *Journal of Southern History*, XXXVIII (May 1972), 216; Arthur S. Link, "Woodrow Wilson: American As Southerner," *Journal of Southern History*, XXXVI (February 1970), 3–17; Dewey Grantham, ed., *The South and the Sectional Image: The Sectional Theme Since Reconstruction* (New York: Harper & Row, Publishers, 1967), passim; Frank Vandiver, ed., *The Idea of the South* (Chicago: University of Chicago Press, 1964), passim.

3. Mobile *Register*, February 24, 1899; W. H. S. Burgwyn to Walter Clark, September 17, 1906 in *Papers of Walter Clark*, II, 82–83.

4. Taylor, "Reminiscences [of Hannis Taylor]," 8–9; interview with Mary L. Taylor Hunt, December 28, 1971.

Bibliography

I. The Writings of Hannis Taylor

Books:

Cicero: A Sketch of His Life and Works. Chicago: A. C. McClung, 1916.

Constitutional Crisis in Great Britain. Concord, N.H.: The Rumford Press, 1910.

Due Process of Law and Equal Protection of the Law. Chicago: Callahan and Co., 1917.

Jurisdiction and Procedure of the Supreme Court of the United States. Rochester: Lawyers' Co-operative Publishing Co., 1905.

Origin and Growth of the English Constitution. Boston: Houghton Mifflin Co., 1911.

Origin and Growth of the English Constitution. 2 vols. Boston: Houghton Mifflin Co., 1889, 1898.

The Science of Jurisprudence. New York: Macmillan Co., 1908.

A Treatise on International Public Law. Chicago: Callahan and Co., 1901.

Articles and Pamphlets:

"Alabama," in Vol. I of *Encyclopaedia Britannica.* 10th ed. 26 vols. Edinburgh: Britannica Co., 1902–1903.

"The American Commonwealth." Commencement Address, Georgetown University School of Law, June 4, 1912. Printed in *Congressional Record*, 62nd Cong., 2nd Sess., (1912), 333–35.

"American Law of Impeachment." *North American Review*, CLXXX (April 1905), 502–12.

"An Appeal to Congress to Prevent the Sending of the Conscripted National Militia to European Battle Fields." *Congressional Record*, 65th Cong., 1st Sess. (1917), 640–43.

"Appointment of Honorable Henry D. Clayton as Senator from the State of Alabama." Senate Document 170, 63rd Cong., 1st Sess. (1913), 3–8.

"A Bancroftian Invention." *Yale Law Journal*, XVIII (December 1908), 75–84.

"A Blow at the Freedom of the Press." *North American Review*, CLV (December 1892), 694–705.

"Christmas Eve." Mobile *Register*, December 24, 1878.

"Comparative Study of Roman and English Law." *Proceedings of Louisiana Bar Association, 1898–99*. New Orleans: Grabner Press, 1899.

"Congo: A Free State." *American Law Review*, XLI (January 1907), 102–07.

"Conquered Territory and the Constitution." *North American Review*, CLXXIII (November 1901), 577–93.

"Constitutional Nationalism." *American Law Review*, XLI (November 1907), 892–900.

"The Designer of the Constitution of the United States." *North American Review*, CLXXXV (August 1907), 813–24.

"Due Process of Law." *American Law Review*, XLI (May 1907), 354–63.

"Due Process of Law." *Yale Law Journal*, XXIV (March 1915), 353–69.

"Elasticity of Written Constitutions." *North American Review*, CLXXXII (February 1906), 204–14.

"Empire Never Waits." *The Illustrated American*, XXIII (January–June 1898), 8–9.

"England's Colonial Empire." *North American Review*, CLXII (June 1896), 682–97.

"Failure of Spain's Colonial Policy." Mobile *Register*, April 2, 1898.

"Fathers of the Revolution." Speech delivered at Patriot's Day Celebration, Boston, Massachusetts, April 15, 1899. Printed in Mobile *Register*, April 20, 1899.

"Five Master-Builders of the American Commonwealth." *Second Safe and Sane Celebration of Independence Day at the National Capital*. Washington: Superintendent of Documents, 1910.

The Freedom of the Press in the Supreme Court of the United States. Argument of Hannis Taylor. Washington: Judd Publishing Co., [1892].

"Edward A. Freeman." *Yale Review*, II (August 1893), 159–72.

"Genesis of the Supreme Court." *Case and Comment*, XVIII (June 1911), 3–7.

"A Government of Law As Distinguished from a Government of Functionaries." *The Green Bag*, XVIII (June 1906), 489–95.

"The Growing Conception of Neutrality." *American Law Review*, XL (March–April 1906), 252–59.

"Growing Importance of the Fourteenth Amendment." *American Law Review*, XLI (July 1907), 550–60.

"Growth of Hague Ideals." *American Law Review*, XL (January–February 1906), 1–8.

Historical Origins of the Representative System. Mobile, Ala.: The Office of the Mobile *Register*, 1884.

"The House of Representatives and the House of Commons." *North American Review*, CLIX (August 1894), 225–34.

"Ideal School of Politics and Jurisprudence." *North American Review*, CLXXV (October 1902), 461-72.

"The Impending Conflict." *North American Review*, CLXXXIII (July 1906), 24-33.

"Independence of the Federal Judiciary." *American Law Review*, XL (July-August 1906), 481-95.

"Inefficiency of Congress As a Legislative Body." *Proceedings of the Alabama Bar, 1886*. Montgomery: Barrett Printers, 1887.

"International Arbitration and the Pan American Conference." *North American Review*, CLXXIV (March 1902), 303-14.

"International Arbitration: The Product of the Modern International System." *The Green Bag*, XVII (February 1905), 98-104.

"International Conference at Rio de Janeiro." *American Law Review*, XL (November-December 1906), 896-907.

"An Interstate Code Commission." *Proceedings of the Alabama Bar, 1881*. Montgomery: Barrett Printers, 1882.

"Is Colonization A Crime?" *North American Review*, CLXXXIII (October 1906), 737-44.

"Is the Draft Law Constitutional?" *Lafollette's Magazine*, IX (June 1917), 4-5. Reprinted in *Congressional Record*, 65th Cong., 1st Sess. (1917), 354-56.

"The Jurisprudence of Latin America." *Virginia Law Review*, I (October 1913), 1-18.

"Legitimate Functions of the Judge-Made Law." *The Green Bag*, XVII (October 1905), 561-65.

Let Us Return to the Faith of Our Fathers. Washington: [n.p.], 1919.

"The Lincoln-Douglas Debates and Their Application to Present Problems." *North American Review*, CLXXXIX (February 1909), 161-73.

"Lord Haldine and the Monroe Doctrine." *Georgetown Law Journal*, II (June 1914), 1-5.

Loyalty to the Constitution. [n.p.], 1917.

"Minnesota Rate Cases." *Harvard Law Review*, XVII (November 1913), 14-26.

"Municipal Charters—The Power to Repeal Them." Mobile *Register*, November 17, 1878.

"National Boundaries." *American Law Review* XL (August 1906), 750-57.

"National House of Representatives." *Atlantic Monthly*, LXV (June 1890), 766-73.

"National Maritime Rights and Responsibilities in Time of War." *North American Review*, CLXXXI (August 1905), 161-68.

"National Militia Cannot Be Sent Abroad." Mobile *Register*, May 8, 1917. Reprinted in *Congressional Record*, 65th Cong., 3rd Sess. (1917), 6632-33.

"Neutral Territorial Waters As a Naval Base." *American Law Review*, XL (May–June 1906), 402–08.

"A New Era in Legal Government." *North American Review*, CLXXXIX (May 1909), 641–50.

"Noteworthy Changes in Statute Law." *Proceedings of the Alabama Bar Association, 1891*. Mobile: Brown Printing Co., 1891.

"The 125th Anniversary of the Drafting of the Constitution of the United States." *Georgetown Law Journal*, I (November 1912), 1–16.

"Origin and Growth of the International System." *Proceedings of the United States Naval Institute, 1902*. Annapolis: The War College, 1902.

"Origin and Growth of the Law of Neutrality." *Georgetown Law Journal*, III (March 1915), 1–7.

"Our Rights and Duties As a Neutral Nation." *Proceedings of the Alabama Bar Association, 1915*. Montgomery: Paragon Press, 1915.

"Our Widening Destiny." Commencement Address at the University of North Carolina, June 1898, printed in Raleigh *News and Observer*, December 23, 1898.

"Outlook for Parliamentary Government." *North American Review*, CLX (April 1895), 479–91.

"The Panama Canal: The Doctrine of *Rebus Sic Stantibus*." *Georgetown Law Journal*, I (May 1913), 193–201.

"The Papacy As an International Power." *American Law Review*, XLI (September 1907), 720–28.

"The Pending Appeal of the American People to Sign Their Own Death Warrant." *Congressional Record*, 66th Cong., 1st Sess. (1919), 4722–25.

"Pending Problems." *North American Review*, CLXVII (November 1898), 609–24.

"The People Must Decide." *Congressional Record*, 65th Cong., 3rd Sess. (1919), 3657–58.

"Petition . . . Presented to Congress . . . on the One-hundred and Thirty-first Anniversary of the Publication of . . . Pelatiah Webster's Tract." *Congressional Record*, 63rd Cong., 2nd Sess. (1914), 3588–91.

"The Place of the New World in the Family of Nations." Commencement Address, University of Alabama, June 19, 1900. Printed in Mobile *Register*, June 29, 1900.

"A Political History of the State [of Alabama]," in Vol. I of *Memorial Record of Alabama*. 2 vols. Madison, Wis.: Brant and Fuller, 1893.

"Powers of the French President." *North American Review*, CLXIV (February 1897), 129–38.

"Reply to Plagiarism." *Law Notes*, XII (June 1909), 59–60.

"Representative Government for Russia." *North American Review*, CLXXX
    (January 1905), 19–27.
"Retrocession Act of 1846." Senate Document 286, 61st Cong., 2nd Sess.,
    1910.
"Review of the Cuban Question in Its Economic, Political, and Diplomatic
    Aspects." *North American Review*, CLXV (November 1897), 610–35.
A Review of President Wilson's Administration. Washington: [n.p.], 1916.
"Roman and English Law As Great World Systems." Address before South
    Carolina Bar Association, printed in full in Columbia, South Carolina
    State, January 23, 1910.
"Abram J. Ryan," in Vol. X of *Library of Southern Literature*. 17 vols. Atlanta:
    Martin and Hoyt Co., 1903–1913.
"Science of Jurisprudence." *Harvard Law Review*, XXII (February 1909),
    241–49.
Shall We Perpetuate the Wilson Dictatorship As a System of Government?
    Washington: [n.p.], 1916.
"The Solid South: A National Calamity." *North American Review*, CLXXXIX
    (January 1909), 1–10.
"Spain's Political Future." *North American Review*, CLXVI (June 1898), 686–
    96.
"The Spanish Treaty Claims Commission." *North American Review*,
    CLXXXII (May 1906), 738–46.
"Speaker and His Powers." *North American Review*, CLXXXVIII (October
    1908), 495–503.
"The Speaker's Tyranny." *New York Times*, November 19, 1890.
Speech to Confederate Veterans, printed in Montgomery *Advertiser*, June 4,
    1901.
"Spheres of Influence and Protectorates." *American Law Review*, XLI (January
    1907), 92–101.
"Startling Growth of State Power." *North American Review*, CXC (October
    1909), 454–63.
"Those Gifts to Mr. Wilson." *Congressional Record*, 66th Cong., 1st Sess.
    (1919), 4725.
"Triumph of American Diplomacy." *National Republican*, April 22, 29, 1922.
    Also printed privately and printed in *Congressional Record*, 67th Cong.,
    2nd Sess. (1922), 7888–95.
"True Remedy for Lynch Law." *American Law Review*, XLI (March 1907),
    255–66.
"The Two Great Canals." *National Waterways: A Magazine of Transportation*, I
    (November 1912), 105–10. Reprinted in *Congressional Record*, 62nd
    Cong., 1st Sess. (1908), 5630–38.

"Unification of American Law." *The Green Bag*, XXII (May 1910), 267–74.
"Vivid Pictures of Old Times in New Bern," *North Carolina Review*, August 7, 1910.
"Pelatiah Webster: Architect of Our Federal Constitution." *Yale Law Journal*, XVII (December 1907), 73–85.
"Pelatiah Webster's Plan of the Constitution." *Congressional Record*, 60th Cong., 1st Sess. (1908), 5630–38.
"Petition Presented to Congress...On the Anniversary of Pelatiah Webster's Epoch-making Tract." *Congressional Record*, 63rd Cong., 2nd Sess., 3588–91.
"What We Owe to the Magna Charta." *New York Times*, June 13, 1915.
Why the Pending Treaty With Colombia Should Be Ratified. Washington: [n.p.], 1914. Reprinted in *Congressional Record*, 63rd Cong., 2nd Sess. (1914), 12369–72.
"Work of the Peace Commission." *North American Reivew*, CLXVII (December 1898), 744–51.

II. Personal Manuscript Collections

Herbert Baxter Adams Papers. Milton S. Eisenhower Library, The Johns Hopkins University, Baltimore, Maryland.
Baldwin Family Papers. Manuscripts Division, Yale University Library, New Haven, Connecticut.
Battle Family Papers. Southern Historical Collection, University of North Carolina, Chapel Hill, North Carolina.
Grover Cleveland Papers. Manuscripts Division, Library of Congress, Washington, D.C.
Erwin Craighead Papers. In possession of Caldwell Delaney, Mobile, Alabama.
Nathaniel H. R. Dawson Papers. Southern Historical Collection, University of North Carolina, Chapel Hill, North Carolina.
Jacob M. Dickinson Papers. Manuscripts Division, Tennessee State Archives, Nashville, Tennessee.
James Gibbons Papers. Archives of the Archdiocese of Baltimore, Chancery Building, Baltimore, Maryland.
Peter Joseph Hamilton Papers. Manuscripts Division, Alabama State Department of Archives and History, Montgomery, Alabama.
Hilary Herbert Papers. Southern Historical Collection, University of North Carolina, Chapel Hill, North Carolina.
Oliver Wendell Holmes Papers. Harvard Law School Library, Harvard University, Cambridge, Massachusetts.

Hunt-McWilliams Correspondence. Letters written by Mary L. Taylor Hunt to Tennant S. McWilliams, and in possession of Tennant S. McWilliams, Birmingham, Alabama.

Joseph F. Johnston Governor's Papers. Manuscripts Division, Alabama State Department of Archives and History, Montgomery, Alabama.

Thomas Goode Jones Papers. Manuscripts Division, Alabama State Department of Archives and History, Montgomery, Alabama.

Henry Cabot Lodge Papers. Manuscripts Division, Massachusetts Historical Society, Boston, Massachusetts.

William McKinley Papers. Manuscripts Division, Library of Congress, Washington, D.C.

Moore-McWilliams Correspondence. Letters written by Elizabeth Moore to Tennant S. McWilliams, in possession of Tennant S. McWilliams, Birmingham, Alabama.

John Tyler Morgan Papers. Manuscripts Division, Library of Congress, Washington, D.C.

R. A. Nunn Papers. In possession of Elizabeth Moore, New Bern, North Carolina.

Richard Olney Papers. Manuscripts Division, Library of Congress, Washington, D.C.

Matt W. Ransom Papers. Southern Historical Collection, University of North Carolina, Chapel Hill, North Carolina.

John Rapier Correspondence. In possession of Reginia Rapier Marston, Mobile, Alabama.

F. C. Roberts Papers. In possession of Elizabeth Moore, New Bern, North Carolina.

Cornelia Phillips Spencer Papers. Southern Historical Collection, University of North Carolina, Chapel Hill, North Carolina.

Hannis Taylor Correspondence. In possession of Mrs. Gossett McRae, Mobile, Alabama.

Applications and Recommendations for Office: Hannis Taylor. Civil Archives Division, National Archives, Washington, D.C.

Issac Taylor Papers. Southern Historical Collection, University of North Carolina, Chapel Hill, North Carolina.

Tucker Family Papers. Southern Historical Collection, University of North Carolina, Chapel Hill, North Carolina.

Washington Family Papers. In possession of Elizabeth Moore, New Bern, North Carolina.

Henry Watterson Papers. Manuscripts Division, Library of Congress, Washington, D.C.

III. Documents

Federal:

Malloy, William M., compiler. *Treaties, Conventions, International Acts, Protocols, and Other Agreements Between the United States of America and Other Powers, 1776–1909.* Washington: Government Printing Office, 1910.

United States Census Bureau. *Manuscript Returns on the United States Seventh Census, 1850.* National Archives: National Archives Microfilm Publications, 1954.

——. *United States Ninth Census. Statistics for the Population of the United States.* Washington: Government Printing Office, 1872.

United States Congress. *Congressional Record.* 49th Cong. (1886); 63rd Cong. (1913)–67th Cong. (1923).

——. 58th Cong., 2nd Sess., Senate Document 162, Alaskan Boundary Tribunal. *Proceedings of the Alaskan Boundary Tribunal.* 7 vols. Washington: Government Printing Office, 1904.

——. *Statutes At Large.* Vol. XXVI.

United States Department of Justice. Case File on *Cox v. Wood.* Civil Archives Division, National Archives, Washington, D.C.

——. Notes of Meetings of the Spanish Treaty Claims Commission Made by William E. Chandler, 1901–1907. Civil Archives Division, National Archives, Washington, D.C.

——. Spain: Claims, 1901—Miscellaneous Correspondence of William E. Chandler Regarding the Spanish Treaty Claims Commission, 1901–1907. Civil Archives Division, National Archives, Washington, D.C.

——. Spanish Treaty Claims Commission. *Final Report of William Wallace Brown.* Washington: Government Printing Office, 1910.

——. Spanish Treaty Claims Commission. *Final Report of William E. Fuller.* Washington: Government Printing Office, 1907.

United States Department of State. *Foreign Relations of the United States, 1893–1897.* Washington: Government Printing Office, 1894–1898.

——. Records of the Foreign Service Posts of the Department of State: Spain—Miscellaneous Letters, XXXII, May 1, 1897–June 20, 1898. Civil Archives Division, National Archives, Washington, D.C.

——. *Register of the Department of State.* Washington: Government Printing Office, 1897.

——. Spain: Despatches. CXVII–CXXXI, April 18, 1893–September 29, 1897. Civil Archives Division, National Archives, Washington, D.C.

Microfilm copies of these documents are included in National Archives Microfilm Publications, Microcopy No. 31, rolls 118–22.

———. Spain: Instructions. XXI–XXII, March 9, 1891–March 9, 1900. Civil Archives Division, National Archives, Washington, D.C. Microfilm copies of these documents are included in National Archives Microfilm Publications, Microcopy No. 77, rolls 149–50.

United States Supreme Court. Attorney Rolls of the United States Supreme Court: List of Attorneys and Counsellors Admitted to Practice in the Supreme Court of the United States, 1790–1886. Civil Archives Division, National Archives, Washington, D.C. Microfilm copies of these documents are included in National Archives Microfilm Publications, Microcopy No. 217.

———. United States Supreme Court Dockets. Civil Archives Division, National Archives, Washington, D.C. Microfilm copies of these documents are included in National Archives Microfilm Publications, Microcopy No. 216.

———. United States Supreme Court Minutes. Civil Archives Division, National Archives, Washington, D.C. Microfilm copies of these documents are included in National Archives Microfilm Publications, Microcopy No. 215.

———. United States Supreme Court Dockets. Civil Archives Division,

State and County:

Baldwin County, Alabama. Commissions of Baldwin County, 1862–1882. Alabama State Department of Archives and History, Montgomery, Alabama.

Craven County, North Carolina. Deed Register of Craven County. Office of the County Clerk, New Bern, North Carolina.

State of Alabama General Assembly. *Acts of the General Assembly of Alabama, 1890–1891.* Montgomery: Roemer Printing Co., 1891.

State of Alabama Senate. *Senate Journal, 1890–91.* Montgomery: Brown Printing Co., 1891.

State of Alabama Supreme Court. *Alabama Reports.* Vols. XLVIII–LVIII, LXXVII, LXXXIV, and XCVIII.

———. Clerk's Docket. Alabama Supreme Court Library, Judicial Building, Montgomery, Alabama.

———. Alabama Supreme Court Roll of Attorneys and Solicitors. Alabama Supreme Court Library, Judicial Building, Montgomery, Alabama.

———. Minutes of the Alabama Supreme Court, 1871–1872. Alabama Supreme Court Library, Judicial Building, Montgomery, Alabama.

University of North Carolina Faculty Minutes [for 1867] Southern Historical
Collection, University of North Carolina, Chapel Hill, North Carolina.
University [of North Carolina] Student Records, 1852–1868. Southern His-
torical Collection, University of North Carolina, Chapel Hill, North
Carolina.

Private:

Records of Historic Mobile Preservation Society. Oakleigh House, Mobile,
Alabama.
Records of the Philanthropic Society [of the University of North Carolina].
Southern Historical Collection, University of North Carolina, Chapel
Hill, North Carolina.
St. Joseph's Church Baptismal Records. Rectory, St. Joseph's Church,
Mobile, Alabama.
St. Matthew's Church Register of Deaths. Rectory, St. Matthew's Church,
Washington, D.C.
Taylor Family Records. Taylor Family Bible, in possession of the heirs of
Mrs. J. Lloyd Abbot, Mobile, Alabama.

IV. Unpublished Manuscripts

Beverly, Frances. "Hannis Taylor." Typewritten MS in Records of Historic
Mobile Preservation Society, Oakleigh House, Mobile, Alabama.
Decker, Joe Frank. "Progressive Reaction to Selective Service in World War
I." Ph.D. dissertation, University of Georgia, 1969.
Dyer, Thomas G. "Theodore Roosevelt and the Idea of Race." Ph.D.
dissertation, University of Georgia, 1975.
Faile, Erwin C. "Thomas Greene Bush: Alabama Spokesman of the New
South." M.A. thesis, Auburn University, 1967.
Foreman, Mrs. Alexander. "Hospitals of Mobile." Typewritten MS in Man-
uscripts Collection, Museum of the City of Mobile, Mobile, Alabama.
Girling, Martha Ashley. "Southern Attitudes Toward the Cuban Craze."
M.A. thesis, Mississippi State University, 1960.
Harris, David Alan. "Racists and Reformers: A Study of Progressivism in
Alabama, 1896–1911." Ph.D. dissertation, University of North
Carolina, 1967.
Herbert, Hilary. "Grandfather Talks About His Life Under Two Flags."
MS in Hilary Herbert Papers, Southern Historical Collection, Univer-
sity of North Carolina, Chapel Hill, North Carolina.
Hollister, Mary Bryan. Untitled typed MS on Taylor family in Issac Taylor

Papers. Southern Historical Collection, University of North Carolina, Chapel Hill, North Carolina.

Hunt, Mary L. Taylor. "Memoirs of a Diplomat's Daughter." Typewritten MS in possession of Tennant S. McWilliams, Birmingham, Alabama.

Langham, Inez Perry. "Politics in Mobile County, 1890–1900." M.A. thesis, University of Alabama, 1947.

Offner, John L. "President McKinley and the Origins of the Spanish-American War." Ph.D. dissertation, Pennsylvania State University, 1957.

Radke, August C. "John Tyler Morgan, Expansionist Senator, 1877–1907." Ph.D. dissertation, University of Washington, 1954.

Taylor, Alfred R. "Reminiscences [of Hannis Taylor]." Untyped MS in Southern Historical Collection, University of North Carolina, Chapel Hill, North Carolina.

"Hannis Taylor." Unidentified typed sketch in Records of Historic Mobile Preservation Society. Oakleigh House, Mobile, Alabama.

Taylor, Richard V. "A Voice from Alabama: An Autobiography Which Includes a Record of a Journey from a Cooper's Bench to a Seat on the Interstate Commerce Commission." Typewritten MS in possession of the heirs of Mrs. J. Lloyd Abbot, Mobile, Alabama.

Washington, Maud M., Compiler. "John N. Washington." Typed MS in Washington Family Papers. In possession of Elizabeth Moore, New Bern, North Carolina.

V. Letters to the Author

Mildren S. Coley, Montgomery, Alabama, February 22, 1972.

Caldwell Delaney, Mobile, Alabama, July 17, 1972.

Blase Dixon, Washington, D.C., March 25, April 23, 1972.

Monsignor John F. Donoghue, Washington, D.C., July 31, 1972.

John A. S. Grenville. Birmingham, England, January 26, 1972.

Roxana Henson, Washington, D.C., February 14, 1972.

Milo B. Howard, Jr., Montgomery, Alabama, March 3, 1972.

Monsignor John K. Kuhn, Washington, D.C., May 16, 1972.

Lela Legaré, Montgomery, Alabama, February 17, 1972.

Reginia Rapier Marston, Mobile, Alabama, March 24, 1972.

David Mathews, Sr., Grove Hill, Alabama, June 26, 1972.

H. Wayne Morgan, Austin, Texas, January 12, 1972.

Paul L. Murphy, Minneapolis, Minnesota, December 5, 1972.

Susan Murray, Washington, D.C., September 19, 1966.

Palmer Pillans, Mobile, Alabama, February 29, June 20, 1972.

Rex G. Rapier, Mobile, Alabama, March 14, 1972.
Jon Reynolds, Washington, D.C., March 7, 1972.
T. Herndon Smith, Mobile, Alabama, March 3, 1972.
State of North Carolina Department of Archives and History, Raleigh,
    North Carolina, August 22, 1972.
Lily M. Swann, Washington, D.C., June 30, 1972.
Walter W. Wright, Hanover, New Hampshire, August 16, 1972.

VI. Interviews

Mrs. J. Lloyd Abbot, Mobile, Alabama, February 24, 1972.
Mary L. Taylor Hunt, Boston, Massachusetts, December 28, 1971.
Monsignor Oscar H. Lipscomb, Mobile, Alabama, February 25, 1972.
Palmer Pillans, Mobile, Alabama, February 22, 1972.

VII. Newspapers

During the mid to late nineteenth century, the Mobile *Register* was a cosmopolitan, carefully prepared newspaper that covered foreign affairs as closely as state and local developments. It was a New South journal in the mold of the *Atlanta Constitution* and the *Charlotte Daily Observer*. Edited by Hannis Taylor's close friend, John L. Rapier, the *Register* chronicled Taylor's entire career, from his rise to prominence in Mobile during the 1870s to his death in Washington, D.C. in 1922. Taylor's political activities at the turn of the century can also be traced in several other Alabama papers: the Birmingham *Age-Herald* (1900–1901), the *Clarke County Democrat* (1898), the Jackson *South Alabamian* (1898, 1900), the *Montgomery Advertiser* (1900–1901), and the *Montgomery Journal* (1900–1901). Beyond his home state, Taylor's emergence as an established scholar, an ambitious lawyer, and a publicist of progressivism was covered, with unmistakable tones of New South boosterism, in the New Orleans *Times-Democrat* (1895), the *Raleigh News and Observer* (1892–1898), and the *Atlanta Constitution* (1897–1900). National papers—the *New York Herald* (1919), the New York *Journal* (1897), the *New York Times* (1890–1922), and the *Washington Post* (1897–1922)—usually gave more balanced assessments of Taylor's significance on a given occasion. For his role as a diplomat and as a critic of foreign policy, the *New York Times* (1890–1919) and the *London Times* (1896–1903) provided consistent and often detailed coverage; and with rare exception, the Mobile *Register* reprinted pertinent foreign-policy articles from these larger papers and then commented on them. London's *Pall Mall Gazette* (1897) and *Standard* (1896) also helped provide detail on Taylor's complicated activities in Spanish-American diplomacy.

VIII. Memoirs, Autobiographies, and Published Correspondence and Published Correspondence and Papers

The Cabinet Diaries of Josephus Daniels (Lincoln, Nebr.: University of Nebraska Press, 1963), ed. by E. David Cronon, and Charles E. Dawes's *Journal of the McKinley Years* (Chicago: Lakeside Press, 1950) yielded a few tidbits useful in piecing together the complicated features of Taylor's personality. Much more important in this respect was Mary L. Taylor Hunt's "Memoirs of a Diplomat's Daughter," a typed manuscript giving the remembrances of Hannis Taylor's oldest daughter; this was written in 1966 at the author's request and remains in his possession. Shorter, though equally revealing, was Alfred R. Taylor's "Remembrances [of Hannis Taylor]," an untyped manuscript written by Hannis Taylor's oldest son and located in the Southern Historical Collection, University of North Carolina.

Two autobiographies written by well-known citizens of south Alabama also were very useful, not just in what they gave on Hannis Taylor but in what they reflected about Alabama during the late nineteenth and early twentieth centuries. Richard V. Taylor's "A Voice from Alabama: An Autobiography Which Includes a Record of a Journey from a Cooper's Bench to a Seat on the Interstate Commerce Commission" is the provocative 400-page typescript left by Hannis Taylor's younger brother, who was an executive with the Mobile and Ohio Railroad as well as the perennial mayor of Mobile; the manuscript remains in possession of the heirs of Mrs. J. Lloyd Abbot, Mobile, Alabama, and should be published. Equally candid (and verbose) is *To Inquiring Friends—If Any: The Autobiography of [Judge] John McDuffie* (Mobile: Azalea Printers, 1969), ed. by Mary Margaret Flock.

Some of the better known national collections of correspondence and papers also proved useful. *Selections from the Correspondence of Henry Cabot Lodge and Theodore Roosevelt* (2 vols., New York: Charles Scribner's Sons, 1925) helped relate Taylor's foreign-policy ideas to those of two noted Republican expansionists. Taylor's connection with the Johns Hopkins "scientific" scholarship as well as with the evolutionary naturalism of late nineteenth-century historiography was illuminated in *Historical Scholarship in the United States, 1876–1901, As Revealed in the Correspondence of Herbert Baxter Adams*, ed. by W. Stull Holt, in *The Johns Hopkins University Studies in History and Political Science*, Series LVI, No. 4 (Baltimore: Johns Hopkins University Press, 1938). Mark DeWolfe Howe's *Holmes-Laski Letters* (2 vols., Cambridge: Harvard University Press, 1941) and *Holmes-Pollack Letters* (2 vols., Cambridge: Harvard University Press, 1941) contain a limited number of references to Taylor, but they assisted immeasurably in judging Taylor's significance as a lawyer and legal scholar. Other collections that proved helpful include *Letters of Grover Cleveland* (Boston: Houghton Mifflin Co., 1933), ed. by Allan Nevins; *Letters of Theodore Roosevelt* (8 vols., Cambridge: Harvard University Press, 1951–1954), ed. by Elting E. Morison; and *Papers of Walter Clark* (2 vols., Chapel Hill: University of North Carolina Press, 1950), ed. by Aubry Lee Brooks and Hugh Talmadge Lefler.

IX. Biographies

For over twenty years Hannis Taylor lived on the fringes of power and, as indicated in Personal Manuscript Collections cited above, he communicated with numerous eminent Americans. Because Taylor never actually made it into the power circles, however, most biographers working in Hannis Taylor's era had no need to make reference to Taylor even when they encountered him in their research. A few did help in linking Taylor with the Republican expansionist diplomacy: Royal Cortissoz, *Life and Letters of Whitelaw Reid* (2 vols., New York: Charles Scribner's Sons, 1921); Allan Nevins, *Henry White* (New York: Dodd, Mead & Co., 1950); Leonard Burr Richardson, *William E. Chandler, Republican* (New York: Dodd, Mead & Co., 1940); and William Rascoe Thayer, *The Life and Letters of John Hay* (2 vols., Boston: Houghton Mifflin Co., 1908). Three other biographies set in the late nineteenth and early twentieth centuries make no mention of Taylor but still influenced the author by demonstrating "the times" interwoven with the personality in scholarly analysis: William F. Holmes, *The White Chief: James Kimble Vardaman* (Baton Rouge: Louisiana State University Press, 1969); Dewey Grantham, *Hoke Smith and the Politics of the New South* (Baton Rouge: Louisiana State University Press, 1958); and Joseph L. Morrison, *Josephus Daniels: Small-d Democrat* (Chapel Hill: University of North Carolina Press, 1966).

X. Articles and Essays

The following articles and essays have useful information on Hannis Taylor chiefly as a historian and diplomat: E. Wilder Spaulding, "Hannis Taylor," in Vol. XVII of *Dictionary of American Biography* (22 vols., New York: Charles Scribner's Sons, 1936); "Hannis Taylor," in Vol. VIII of *National Cyclopaedia of American Biography* (13 vols., New York: James T. White and Co., 1900); William Burlie Brown, "The State Literary and History Association, 1900–1950," *North Carolina Historical Review*, XXVIII (April 1951), 156–97; William A. Dunning, Review of *Origin and Growth of the English Constitution, Political Science Quarterly*, V (March 1890), 188–90; Earl of Meath, "Anglo-Saxon Unity," *Fortnightly Review*, CCLXXXIX (April 1891),

144 BIBLIOGRAPHY

615-22; "Ex-Minister Taylor on Cuba," *Nation*, LXV (November 4, 1897), 350-51; John Fiske, "An American History of the Enlgish Constitution," *Atlantic Monthly*, LXV (February 1890), 263-66; Henry L. Goody, "Plagiarism—A Fine Art," *Juridical Review*, XX (January 1909), 302-15; W. C. Jackson, "Culture and the New Era in North Carolina," *North Carolina Historical Review*, II (January 1925), 3-18; Roscoe Pound, "Taylor's *Science of Jurisprudence*; A Literary Application of the Doctrine of Accession," *Illinois Law Review*, III (March 1909), 302-15; James R. Randall, "Sketch of Our New Minister to Spain," *Church News*, reprinted in Mobile *Register*, June 11, 1893; John L. Stewart, Review of *Origin and Growth of the English Constitution*, in *Annals of American Academy of Political and Social Science*, I (July 1890), 145-47; William P. Trent, "Notes on Recent Work in Southern History," *Proceedings of the Virginia Historical Society*, XI (December 1891), 47-60.

Short studies that provide background for Hannis Taylor's North Carolina youth and his emergence as a publicist of conservative Democracy in Alabama include Horace Mann Bond's still authoritative "Social and Economic Forces During Reconstruction in Alabama," *Journal of Negro History*, XXIII (July 1938), 336-43; Allen J. Going, "The South and the Blair Bill," *Mississippi Valley Historical Review*, XLIV (September 1957), 267-90; and William H. Oliver, comp., "Centennial Commemoration of New Bern Academy" (New Bern, 1906). On the conceptual framework for Taylor's role as a diplomat and as a New South expansionist, see O. Lawrence Burnette, Jr., "John Tyler Morgan and Expansionist Sentiment in the New South," *Alabama Review*, XVIII (July 1965), 163-82; Tennant S. McWilliams, "Petition for Expansion: Mobile Businessmen and the Cuban Crisis, 1898," *Alabama Review*, XXVIII (January 1975), 58-63; Tennant S. McWilliams, "The Lure of Empire: Southern Interest in the Caribbean, 1877-1900," *Mississippi Quarterly*, XXIX (Winter 1975-76), 43-64; and Christopher Lasch, "The Anti-Imperialists, the Philippines, and the Inequality of Man," *Journal of Southern History*, XIV (August 1958), 319-31.

Among the great number of periodical articles that help provide background for Taylor's role as a progressive on the domestic scene, these are of key importance: E. Merton Coulter, "The Attempt of William Howard Taft to Break the Solid South," *Georgia Historical Quarterly*, XIX (June 1935), 134-44; Edward A. Gilmore's "Legislative Co-operation Among the States," *American Bar Association Journal*, VII (February 1921), 74 and Charles P. Sherman's "One Code for All States," *The Green Bag*, XXV (November 1913), 460-67—only two of a massive list of legal writings that used as primary sources, point to the relatively unexplored topic of lawyers, efficiency, and progressivism; Joseph Huthmaker, "Urban Liberalism in the Age of Reform," *Mississippi Valley Historical Review*, XLIX (September 1962), 231-41, characterized below with other studies on the origins of progressivism; Oscar Kraines, "The President Versus the Congress: the Keep Commission, 1905–1909, the First Comprehensive Inquiry into Administration," *Western Political Science Quarterly*, XXIII (March 1970), 5–54; Arthur S. Link, "Woodrow Wilson: American As Southerner," *Journal of Southern History*, XXXVI (February 1970), 3–17; Seth M. Scheiner, "President Theodore Roosevelt and the Negro," *Journal of Negro History*, XLVII (July 1962), 169–82; Dewey W. Grantham, Jr., "The Progressive Movement and the Negro," *South Atlantic Quarterly*, LIV (October 1955), 461–77; Frances B. Simkins, "Ben Tillman's View of the Negro," *Journal of Southern History*, III (May 1937), 161–74.

The progressives' determination to take their reforms beyond the boundaries of the United States, indeed, to uplift the world, is a topic badly in need of rethinking and resynthesis. Nevertheless, a number of important articles helped in understanding Taylor as a progressive looking outward: Thomas A. Bailey, "Theodore Roosevelt and the Alaskan Boundary Settlement," *Canadian Historical Review*, XVIII (June 1937), 123–30; John W. Foster, "The Alaskan Boundary Tribunal," *National Geographic Magazine*, XV (December 1904), 1–12; Charles G. Washburn, "Memoir of Henry Cabot Lodge," *Massachusetts Historical Society Proceedings*, LVIII (1925), 324–76; John P. Campbell, "Taft, Roosevelt, and the Arbitration Treaties of 1911," *Journal of American History*, LIII (September 1966), 279–98; William E. Leuchtenburg, "Progressivism and Imperialism: The Progressive Movement and American Foreign Policy," *Mississippi Valley Historical Review*, XXXIX (December 1952), 483–504; Lloyd C. Gardner, "American Foreign Policy, 1900–1921," in *Towards a New Past: Dissenting Essays in American History*, ed. by Barton Bernstein (New York: Pantheon Books, 1967); John Milton Cooper, Jr., "Progressivism and American Foreign Policy: A Reconsideration," *Mid-America*, LI (October 1969), 260–77; and Arthur S. Link, "The Cotton Crisis, the South and Anglo-American Diplomacy, 1914–1915," in *Studies in Southern History in Memory of Albert Ray Newsome, 1894–1951* (Chapel Hill: University of North Carolina Press, 1957).

XI. General Works

In writing a biography of a secondary figure such as Hannis Taylor, it is critical to relate the subject to the major, broad syntheses of the era; otherwise, the biography amounts to little more than geneaology and antiquarianism. Hence many well-known general works that included little, if any, reference to Hannis Taylor assumed tremendous importance during the research, organization, and writing of this book. Although Taylor does not seem to fit the Woodward hypothesis—that a Southerner might employ the harsh reality of his Southern experience to crack national myths and frame realistic concepts about American life—this author remains one of many individuals interested in the recent South who is indebted to C. Vann Woodward. In *Origins of the New South* (Baton Rouge: Louisiana State University Press, 1951), *The Strange Career of Jim Crow* (New York: Oxford University Press, 1957), and *The Burden of Southern History* (rev. ed., Baton Rouge: Louisiana State University Press, 1970), Woodward suggested and in many cases fully explored key social and psychological implications of the Southern experience. Whether subsequent writings on the South have supported, modified, or refuted Woodward's work, that work has provided a dominant catalyst to recent South scholarship over the past quarter decade. Other major syntheses bearing on Taylor's Southern experience are included in *The Idea of the South: Pursuit of a Central Theme*, ed. by Frank E. Vandiver (Chicago: University of Chicago Press, 1964); *Myth and Southern History*, ed. by Patrick Gerster and Nicholas Cords (2 vols., Chicago: Rand McNally & Co., 1974); *The Southerner As American*, ed. by Charles Grier Sellers, Jr. (Chapel Hill: University of North Carolina Press, 1960); and, a study that gave conceptual underpinnings for Chapter II, Paul M. Gaston's *The New South Creed: A Study in Southern Mythmaking* (New York: Alfred A. Knopf, 1970).

Several specific aspects of the New South experience deserve special note. Woodward's *Origins of the New South* goes a long way toward integrating Southern political trends into national affairs. Also useful here are the well-respected duo, Stanley P. Hirshon, *Farewell to the Bloody Shirt: Northern Republicans and the Southern Negro* (Bloomington: Indiana University Press, 1962); and Vincent P. DeSantis, *Republicans Face the Southern Question: The New Departure Years, 1877-1897* (Baltimore: Johns Hopkins University Press, 1959). The lottery, a fascinating Southern as well as national political issue, and one that dominated Hannis Taylor's legal career for about two years, is explored in John Ezell's careful, readable *Fortune's Merry Wheel: The Lottery in America* (Cambridge: Harvard University Press, 1960). There is also the key issue of the evolution of segregation. Debates as to exactly when and why formal segregation came to the deep South can be traced in *The Origins of Segregation* (Baton Rouge: Louisiana State University Press, 1968), ed. by Joel Williamson; as well as in J. Morgan Kousser's *The Shaping of Southern Politics: Suffrage Restrictions and the Establishment of the One-Party South, 1880-1910* (New Haven and London: Yale University Press, 1974). As to the intellectual and psychological characteristics of American racism, one has an overwhelming amount of material to draw from; and especially useful for Taylor's time period are these: Joel Kovel, *White Racism: A Psychohistory* (New York: Random House, 1970); George M. Frederickson, *The Black Image in the White Mind: The Debate on the Afro-American Character and Destiny* (New York: Harper

& Row, Publishers, 1971); and John S. Haller, *Outcasts from Evolution: Attitudes of Racial Inferiority, 1859–1900* (Urbana: University of Illinois Press, 1971).

If the racial, social, and political setting for Taylor's Southern experience can be defined with fair clarity through major secondary sources, so can his role as a late nineteenth-century nationalist and expansionist. These works, though differing in intepretation, offer detailed accounts of America's rise to world power: Julius W. Pratt, *The Expansionists of 1898: The Acquisition of Hawaii and the Spanish Islands* (Baltimore: Johns Hopkins University Press, 1936); Milton Plesur, *America's Outward Thrust: Approaches to Foreign Affairs, 1865–1890* (DeKalb, Ill.: Northern Illinois University Press, 1971); Ernest May, *Imperial Democracy: The Emergence of America as a World Power* (New York: Harcourt, Brace & World, 1961); Walter LaFeber, *The New Empire: An Interpretation of American Expansion, 1860–1898* (Ithaca, N.Y.: Cornell University Press, 1963); H. Wayne Morgan, *America's Road to Empire: The War With Spain and Overseas Expansion* (New York: John Wiley & Sons, 1965); and John A. S. Grenville and George Berkeley Young, *Politics, Strategy, and American Diplomacy: Studies in Foreign Affairs, 1873–1917* (New Haven: Yale University Press, 1966).

Despite the relatively large number of works on America's late nineteenth-century expansionism, a significant question—one encountered in researching Taylor's life—remains in this area: What was the South's impact, as well as that of other regions, on America's outward thrust? Edward W. Chester's *Sectionalism, Politics, and American Diplomacy* (Metuchen, N.J.: Scarecrow Press, 1975) employs selected votes in Congress to argue that Southern political leaders generally opposed expansionism. Yet this conclusion needs clarification. As several have shown, there was a small but definite strain of formal imperialism in the New South, and there was also a powerful element of "informal" or "open door" expansionism functioning in the region. See, for example, McWilliams, "Lure of Empire," *Mississippi Quarterly*, XXIX, 43–63.

Studies on the progressive movement are multitudinous, especially regarding the problem of what caused it. European sources of the movement are emphasized in Arthur Ekirch, Jr., *Progressivism in America* (New York: New View Points, 1974). Agrarian origins are discussed in John D. Hicks, *The Populist Revolt* (Minneapolis: University of Minnesota Press, 1951); and in Russel B. Nye, *Midwestern Progressive Politics* (East Lansing, Mich.: Michigan State University Press, 1951). For the influence of immigrant labor see, for example, Joseph Huthmaker, "Urban Liberalism in the Age of Reform," *Mississippi Valley Historical Review*, XLIX (September 1962), 231–41. The role of the small businessman is treated in George F. Mowry, *The California Progressives* (Berkeley: University of California Press, 1951); and in Richard

Hofstadter, *The Age of Reform: From Bryan to FDR* (New York: Random House, 1955).

At least two strains characterized corporate progressivism, the brand of reformism espoused by Theodore Roosevelt and also by Hannis Taylor. Some elitists of the business society advocated regulation of corporation practices that would bring order and efficiency to America's increasingly complex industrial life. Those efforts were at times complemented and in other instances frustrated by powerful businessmen who advanced superficial regulatory legislation as token concessions designed to appease less conservative reformers and earnest liberals. Corporate progressivism has been the subject of numerous studies: Samuel P. Hays, *Conservation and the Gospel of Efficiency* (Cambridge: Harvard University Press, 1959); Robert H. Wiebe, *Businessmen and Reform: A Study of the Progressive Movement* (Cambridge: Harvard University Press, 1962); Gabriel Kolko, *The Triumph of Conservatism* (New York: Free Press of Glencoe, 1963); James Weinstein, *The Corporate Ideal in the Liberal State 1900–1918* (Boston: Beacon Press, 1968); John Blum, *The Republican Roosevelt* (Cambridge: Harvard University Press, 1954); and G. Wallace Chessman, *Theodore Roosevelt and the Politics of Power* (Boston: Little, Brown & Co., 1968). When a particular plan for reform actually became policy, its enactment sometimes represented the combined efforts of these divergent elements of progressivism—the theme of David Thelen's provocative *The New Citizenship; Origins of Progressivism in Wisconsin, 1885–1900* (Columbia: University of Missouri Press, 1972). Three syntheses of the progressive era are Robert Wiebe, *The Search for Order 1877–1920* (New York: Hill & Wang, 1967); William L. O'Neill, *The Progressive Years: America Comes of Age* (New York: Dodd, Mead & Co., 1975); and Richard T. Watson, *The Development of National Power, 1900–1919* (Boston: Houghton Mifflin Co., 1976).

Beyond the literature concerned with origins of progressivism, this study benefited, too, from the well-known studies of Theodore Roosevelt and Woodrow Wilson provided by John Blum, Arthur S. Link, and William H. Harbaugh, as cited in the notes. Further, the problem of segregation as a reform, something central to Taylor's concept of progressivism, is explored generally in Jack Temple Kirby's *Darkness at the Dawning: Race and Reform in the Progressive Era* (Philadelphia: J. B. Lippincott Co., 1972). The most penetrating study of Theodore Roosevelt's racial views is Thomas G. Dyer's "Theodore Roosevelt and the Idea of Race" (Ph.D. dissertation, University of Georgia, 1975); this author is indebted to Tom Dyer for permission to read this work as it was being written as well as for his general counseling on evolutionary naturalism. Finally, because Taylor was a lawyer functioning during the progressive era, the topic of attorneys and progressive reform was important throughout this project. There is no adequate treatment of the topic, and a glance at the law journals for the early twentieth century indicated that it is indeed a fertile one. General studies in legal history that set the scene for specific developments in Taylor's career include Loren Beth's *The Development of the American Constitution, 1877–1917* (New York: Harper & Row, Publishers, 1971) and Paul L. Murphy's *The Constitution in Crisis Times, 1918–1969* (New York: Harper & Row, Publishers, 1972). See also Paul L. Murphy, *The Meaning of Freedom of Speech* (Westport, Conn.: Greenwood Press, 1972); Benjamin R. Twiss, *Lawyers and the Constitution: How Laissez-faire Came to the Supreme Court* (New York: Russell & Russell Publishers, 1962); and Arnold M. Paul, *Conservative Crisis and the Rule of Law: Attorneys of Bar and Bench, 1887–1895* (Ithaca, N.Y.: Cornell University Press, 1960).

Just as there is a massive amount of material on progressivism at home, there is a plethora of general works relating to American foreign policy during the progressive years. These works helped in evaluating Taylor's role as a critic of America's "progressive" relations with the world: Howard K. Beale, *Theodore Roosevelt and the Rise of America to World Power* (Baltimore: Johns Hopkins University Press, 1958); David H. Burton, *Theodore Roosevelt: Confident Imperialist* (Philadelphia: University of Pennsylvania Press, 1971); Robert E. Osgood, *Ideals and Self-Interest in American Foreign Relations: The Great Transformation of the Twentieth Century* (Chicago: University of Chicago Press, 1953); Arthur S. Link, *Woodrow Wilson and the Progressive Era, 1910–1917* (New York: Harper & Row, Publishers, 1954); and William A. Williams, *The Tragedy of American Diplomacy* (New York: Delta Publishing Co., 1962). As mentioned above, America's continued outward surge during the progressive years is a topic badly in need of resynthesis from an ideological and psychological standpoint. What Jerry Israel's *Progressivism and the Open Door* (Pittsburgh: University of Pittsburgh Press, 1971) tells about American reformism in China during this time needs also to be told about Americans in other areas of the world, especially the Caribbean.

XII. Studies on North Carolina and Alabama

A sizable amount of material was discovered on Taylor's early years in North Carolina by searching through the well-organized holdings of the Southern Historical Collection of the University of North Carolina. As indicated above, manuscript records of the University were especially helpful. Also useful were John G. Barrett, *The Civil War in North Carolina* (Chapel Hill: University of North Carolina Press, 1963); J. G. deRoulhac Hamilton, *North Carolina Since 1860* (Chicago: Lewis Publishing Co., 1919); and Hope

Summersell Chamberlain, *Old Days in Chapel Hill: Being the Life and Times of Cornelia Phillips Spencer* (Chapel Hill: University of North Carolina Press, 1926).

Since Hannis Taylor matured and developed a career in Alabama—he resided in the state for some thirty years—the author needed to make major demands on Alabama historiography. Results were mixed. There is no in-depth, scholarly study of Alabama that makes use of modern historiographical techniques and themes. Albert B. Moore's *History of Alabama* (Nashville: Benson Printing Co., 1934) is conceptually out of date and emphasizes the pre-1900 period. On the other hand, Virginia Van der Veer Hamilton's *Alabama: A Bicentennial History* (New York: W. W. Norton & Co., 1977) concentrates on post-1900 developments and treats the relationship of race, economics, and politics in an open and sensitive way; her short, thematic volume helps fill the gap in ideas so long left open in the writing of Alabama history. Still useful for the researcher are Thomas M. Owen's *History of Alabama and Dictionary of Alabama Biography* (4 vols., Chicago: S. J. Clarke Publishing Co., 1921); and the *Memorial Record of Alabama* (2 vols., Madison, Wis.: Brant and Fuller, 1893), to which Hannis Taylor contributed.

As for monographs on Alabama, see Walter L. Fleming's *Civil War and Reconstruction in Alabama* (New York: Columbia University Press, 1905), which has endured as a scholarly work despite Dunning-school tones; Sarah Woolfolk Wiggins, *The Scalawag in Alabama Politics, 1865–1881* (University, Ala.: University of Alabama Press, 1977); Allen Johnston Going, *Bourbon Democracy in Alabama* (University, Ala.: University of Alabama Press, 1951); Malcolm C. McMillan, *Constitutional Development in Alabama, 1798–1901: A Study in Politics, the Negro, and Sectionalism* (Chapel Hill: University of North Carolina Press, 1955); Sheldon Hackney, *Populism to Progressivism in Alabama* (Princeton: Princeton University Press, 1969); and William Warren Rogers, *The One-Gallused Rebellion: Agrarianism in Alabama, 1865–1896* (Baton Rouge: Louisiana State University Press, 1970). These works do not contain reference to Hannis Taylor; but they offered details and concepts necessary for placing Taylor into the milieu of Alabama political affairs around the turn of the century.

The city of Mobile, Taylor's home, has a full and varied history as well as a large body of good, locally produced social histories. Caldwell Delaney, Curator at the Museum of the City of Mobile, directed the author to many of these, including Thomas Cooper DeLeon's *Bienville Year Bi-centenary: Mobile Carnivals, 200 years Between 1711 and 1911* (Mobile, [1911?]); Erwin Craighead's *Mobile: Fact and Tradition* (Mobile: Powers Printing Co., 1913); and Craighead's *From Mobile's Past* (Mobile: Powers Printing Co., 1925). Also instructive were Caldwell Delaney's *Craighead's Mobile* (Mobile: The Haunted

Bookshop, 1965) and Charles G. Summersell's *Mobile: History of a Seaport Town* (University, Ala.: University of Alabama Press, 1949). Aside from political discussions in Summersell's work and in Inez Langham's thesis (cited above), the history of politics, economics, and race relations in the port city remains largely untold. This should be rectified, at least for the late nineteenth and early twentieth centuries, by an Auburn University dissertation now in progress, David Alsobrook's study of Mobile and the progressive era.

Index

HANNIS TAYLOR
was typeset in VIP Janson and Compugraphic Bernase
by The Composing Room of Michigan, Inc., Grand Rapids, Michigan,
printed by Thomson-Shore, Inc., Dexter, Michigan,
and bound by John H. Dekker and Sons, Grand Rapids, Michigan.
Book and jacket design: Anna F. Jacobs
Production: Paul R. Kennedy